# CRAZY
## CHRISTIANS

*A Call to Follow Jesus*

# CRAZY
## CHRISTIANS

### A Call to Follow Jesus

## Michael B. Curry

Foreword by Katharine Jefferts Schori

 Morehouse Publishing

NEW YORK · HARRISBURG · DENVER

Unless otherwise noted, the Scripture quotations contained herein are from the New Revised Standard Version Bible, copyright © 1989 by the Division of Christian Education of the National Council of Churches of Christ in the U.S.A. Used by permission. All rights reserved.

Morehouse Publishing, 4775 Linglestown Road, Harrisburg, PA 17112
Morehouse Publishing, 19 East 34th Street, New York, NY 10016
Morehouse Publishing is an imprint of Church Publishing Incorporated.

www.churchpublishing.org

Cover design by Laurie Klein Westhafer
Typeset by Denise Hoff

Library of Congress Cataloging-in-Publication Data

Curry, Michael B.
Crazy Christians a call to follow Jesus / Michael B. Curry; foreword by Katharine Jefferts Schori.
     pages cm
  Includes bibliographical references.
  ISBN 978-0-8192-2885-7 (pbk.) -- ISBN 978-0-8192-2886-4
(ebook) 1. Christian life. I. Title.
  BV4501.3.C86 2013
  248.4--dc23
                        2013011827

*Printed in the United States of America*

# Contents

# Foreword

What does it mean to be a faithful Christian in the twenty-first century? The answer to that question has much to do with what it has always meant to be a friend of Jesus, but there are also aspects of faithfulness that must be ready to respond to the challenge of changing times and contexts. As children of the Most High God, we are made for the beloved community, the reign or commonwealth of God, or God's "kindom" (and yes, that is how I meant to spell it). We are all kin one to another, and not only to other human beings. We are a part—a magnificent part—of the whole of God's creation, and as human beings our vocation is to partner in the transformation of this planet toward that ancient and eternal vision of a healed and reconciled existence. Our tradition has long called that vision the divine dream of *shalom*, a community of peace and justice where all God's created parts live together in harmony. The daily prayer of our hearts reminds us that we are created of stardust to bring celestial possibility into earthly reality: ". . . your kingdom come, . . . on earth as in heaven."

As bishop, Michael Curry has been leading God's people in North Carolina and far beyond since 2000. His leadership is always encouraging the movement toward transformation, and he has a remarkable ability to cast the journey toward the reign of God in image, song, and story that lean into the possibility God has open before us. He is deeply rooted in ancient wisdom, current scholarship, and the hope we know in Jesus, and he shares the clarity of vision for which prophets have always been known.

Read and savor these chapters—read them aloud, even, for their cadences teach as much as the words on the page— read, recite, and sing, too, for the hymnody here will enter your bones and help to transform your heart into the vulnerability and compassion of Jesus. These pages are filled with resonance that can connect you with the deep bones of your own story. Remember and reconnect with those in your own life who have shown you God, as Michael's grandmother so clearly did. Where and with whom are you passing on that open-hearted vision of possibility?

Read, dream, and sing—and discover the spirit at work all around you in unexpected people, places, and invitations. Those invitations emerge in the possibility of the mountaintop, as Bishop Curry names it, and what the Celts call "thin places"—encounters with the Holy One. We are far more likely to discover them "on the road," away from our comfort zones and self-constructed prisons, especially when we travel lightly in service of God's healing and reconciliation. So, as one preacher put it long ago, read yourself full, let the word gather heat within your prayer, then with every particle and pulse of passion within you go and proclaim in word and deed what it means to know God's ever-open possibility and faithfulness, and then let your acts and words go—don't hang on to the need for particular results. The result will be transformation of kin together, though it will likely exceed your expectations and limited vision.

It is indeed a crazy dream, but together, the Body of Christ can most certainly help to build the kingdom, transform brokenness, and renew the face of the earth.

—The Most Rev. Dr. Katharine Jefferts Schori
Presiding Bishop of the Episcopal Church
May 2013

# Preface

I have found that some things stick to you, especially when you're young, and over time they become a part of you. One of the things that stuck to me when I was a high school volunteer for the late senator Robert F. Kennedy in his presidential campaign were these words he liked to quote from George Bernard Shaw: "Some men see things as they are and ask why. I dream things that never were and ask why not." Those words stuck with me. And now, decades later, I suspect the Spirit had something to do with that.

When I was a parish priest in the 1980s serving St. Simon of Cyrene Episcopal Church in Lincoln Heights, Ohio, the late Verna J. Dozier spent a day with us. During the period of Jim Crow segregation, Verna had taught English in the Washington, D.C., public schools. She became a member of the Church of the Saviour there and was greatly influenced by the Rev. Gordon Cosby and his commitment to the kind of radical discipleship that dares truly to follow in the footsteps of Jesus. Verna eventually became an Episcopalian, retired from teaching, and placed her formidable literary skills and knowledge in service of the Word of God and the people of God.

As a result she was able to help us Episcopalians and many other mainline Christians, who tend to be somewhat intimidated by the Bible, begin to engage the Holy Scriptures anew. She did that by getting us to actually read the Scriptures, teaching us to listen for and to hear God's word to us and to begin to dream of a world born of God's loving vision for God's creation and for the whole human family.

I first met Verna the day she visited us at St. Simon of Cyrene. In the 1990s I was able to spend more time with her while serving at St. James' Episcopal Church in Baltimore. It was during this period that Verna published a book on the story and significance of the Bible titled *The Dream of God: A Call to Return.*

*The Dream of God* helped me see that the Bible and indeed our Christian faith and tradition are pointing beyond themselves to the will, the vision, the sublime purposes, the passionate desire of God. Verna wrote that the kingdom or reign of God, which Jesus talked about probably more than anything else, is the realization of God's dream and vision for human life, human society, and all of creation.

That dream of God is in part the motive for God's involvement and God's mission in the life of the world, from the days of the Bible until now. That dream inspired the Hebrew prophets, who used God's thunderous, "Thus saith the Lord," to courageously challenge injustice and mistreatment of the poor. That dream is the reason God came among us in the person of Jesus of Nazareth, who showed us the way to live beyond what often are the nightmares of our own sin-filled human design and into the direction of God's dream. Over time I began to see that being a Christian is not essentially about joining a church or being a nice person, but about following in the footsteps of Jesus, taking his teachings seriously, letting his Spirit take the lead in our lives, and in so doing helping to change the world from our nightmare into God's dream.

At some point I began to view the words Bobby Kennedy had quoted in a new and larger light. "Some men see things as they are and ask why. I dream things that never were and ask why not."

Why not?

Why not a world where no child will ever go to bed hungry again?

Why not a world in which poverty is truly history, a thing of the past?

Why not a world in which every person is treated and valued as a child of God?

Why not a world where we lay down our swords and shields, down by the riverside, to study war no more?

Why not a world reconciled to our God and to each other as children of God and brothers and sisters of one another?

Why not a world that looks less like the nightmare of our human devising and more like the dream of God's creating?

Why not?

We who would be disciples of Jesus are people who have made a commitment to follow his teachings, his manner of life, and the loving and liberating reality of his Spirit in the direction of God's great "why not," in the direction of God's dream.

Of course, people in the days of Jesus thought he was crazy. And people who dare to live the way of Jesus in our own time will also be called crazy. I suspect that is what Jesus was getting at when he said, "If any want to become my followers, let them deny themselves and take up their cross and follow me. For those who want to save their life will lose it, and those who lose their life for my sake, and for the sake of the gospel, will save it" (Mark 8:34-35).

Most of the chapters in this book began as sermons or addresses I preached or delivered over twelve years to the Annual Convention of the Episcopal Diocese of North Carolina. Chapter One, "We Need Some Crazy Christians," began as a sermon I preached on July 7, 2012, at the 77th General Convention of The Episcopal Church.

In the process of writing, re-writing, re-working, and wrestling with these essays, I began to see a message unfolding of God's dream and its summons to live the counter-cultural life of real discipleship—a message of hope for a new and transformed creation. I wish I could say I was always fully conscious of and deeply intentional about forming this message. Sometimes I was, but more often than not the words and ideas kept bubbling up and informing me from an unconscious place. I trust that that process had something to do with the Spirit of God, who I believe a long time ago put words on the lips of a senator running for president, words I have never forgotten.

❊ ❊

The many people who have been blessings in my life, and who have informed and helped to shape much of what is in these pages, are sure and certain evidence of the grace of God. I don't deserve them; I didn't earn them; they have been God's gift. For them and for so many others I truly give God thanks.

For my parents, the Rev. Kenneth S. L. Curry and Dorothy Strayhorn Curry, and for my grandparents, Hezekiah and Nellie Strayhorn and the Rev. Theotis and Carrie Curry, all in glory now, who passed on to me a durable faith that was tested and yet still striving in the crucible of chattel slavery and Jim Crow.

For my family, my wife and best friend, Sharon, and our wonderful daughters, Rachel and Elizabeth; for my sister, Sharon Curry Elliot; for Josephine Robbins, our long-standing and dear family friend; and my godmother, Sister Althea Augustine, CT.

For the Rev. Liz Dowling-Sendor who, like a spiritual director, has patiently edited my writings as a bishop, gently nudging me to written clarity, theological coherence, and spiritual authenticity; and for Nancy Bryan of Church Publishing Inc. who believed, long before it ever occurred to me, that there was something in the message of *Crazy Christians* that might be of help to a wider audience of those who seek to follow Jesus in the twenty-first century.

For the incredible members of the staff of the Episcopal Diocese of North Carolina, with particular and special thanks to and for those who over the years have read, critiqued, and been partners in conversation: Margo Acomb, Sarah Herr, the Rt. Rev. J. Gary Gloster, Canon Marlene Weigert, the Rev. Canon Michael Burkel Hunn, the Rt. Rev. Alfred C. Marble Jr., Summerlee Walter, the Rt. Rev. Anne Hodges-Copple, and the Rev. Canon Marie Fleischer.

For the clergy and people of the Diocese of North Carolina with whom I am privileged to serve Jesus and the world in his name; for the people of St. Philip's Episcopal Church, Buffalo, New York, who helped form me as a human being and as a disciple of Jesus in the Episcopal way of being Christian; for the clergy and people of St. Luke's Episcopal Church and St. Paul's (now the Episcopal Church of St. Paul and St. James), New Haven, Connecticut, and the Church of the Epiphany, Rocky Mount, North Carolina, where I served as a seminarian in the 1970s; for the

Episcopal churches where I was blessed to serve as a priest: St. Stephen's Episcopal Church, Winston-Salem, North Carolina; St. Simon of Cyrene Episcopal Church, Lincoln Heights, Ohio; and St. James' Episcopal Church, Baltimore, Maryland.

These and so many others have been vehicles for and evidence of God's grace in my life. May this book be such a gift for you.

Keep the faith,
+Michael
July 1, 2013
Harriet Beecher Stowe
Pauli Murray

## CHAPTER ONE

# We Need Some Crazy Christians

> Then [Jesus] went home; and the crowd came together again, so that they could not even eat. When his family heard it, they went out to restrain him, for people were saying, "He has gone out of his mind." (Mark 3:19–21)

Jesus "has gone out of his mind." That's what the people say in the New Revised Standard Version of the Bible. The King James Version translates it as, "He is beside himself." The old J.B. Phillips New Testament puts it, "He must be mad!" But my favorite is from the 1995 Contemporary English Version which says, "When Jesus' family heard what he was doing, they thought he was crazy and went to get him under control."

1

Trying to get Jesus "under control" is exactly the problem. Fyodor Dostoyevsky in *The Brothers Karamazov* rightly warns us that the Church and we Christians have often tried to make Jesus tame. We want to manage the Messiah. But this Messiah won't be managed. As Richard Holloway, former Primate of Scotland, once wrote, "Jesus goes on breaking out of all the tombs to which we have consigned him."[1]

So, forgive me for saying it this way, but Jesus was, and is, crazy! And those who would follow him, those who would be his disciples, those who would live as and be the people of the Way, are called to be exactly that—crazy. If you asked me what the Church needs today, I would say this: We need some crazy Christians.

Let's go back to that line, "When Jesus' family heard what he was doing, they thought he was crazy and went to get him under control." I don't want to be too quick to judge Jesus' mother and the whole family. They had good reason to be concerned. The First Letter of Peter tells us something that Jesus had already taught in the Sermon on the Mount: "Do not repay evil for evil or abuse for abuse; but, on the contrary, repay with a blessing" (1 Peter 3:9). That's crazy! In Matthew's gospel, Jesus says, "The greatest among you will be your servant" (Matthew 23:11). That's crazy!

What the world calls wretched, Jesus calls blessed. Blessed are the poor and the poor in spirit. Blessed are the merciful, the compassionate. Blessed are those who hunger and thirst that God's righteous justice might prevail. Blessed are those who work for peace. Blessed are you when you are persecuted just for trying to love and

---

1   John Drane, ed., *The Great Sayings of Jesus: Proverbs, Parables and Prayers* (New York: St. Martin's Press, 1999).

do what is good (Matthew 5:3–11). Jesus said all that in the Sermon on the Mount, to crowds of people. That was crazy. Jesus said, "Love your enemies and pray for those that persecute you" (Matthew 5:44). Jesus was crazy. He prayed while folk were killing him, "Father, forgive them; they know not what they are doing" (Luke 23:34). *Now that's crazy.*

What the Church needs, what this world needs, are some Christians who are as crazy as the Lord. Crazy enough to love like Jesus, to give like Jesus, to forgive like Jesus, to do justice, love mercy, walk humbly with God—like Jesus. Crazy enough to dare to change the world from the nightmare it often is into something closer to the dream that God dreams for it. And for those of us who would follow him, those of us who would be his disciples, those of us who would live as the people of the Way? It might come as a shock, but those of us called to that life are called to craziness, too.

Let me suggest one example of such a call from the New Testament: Mary of Magdala, also known as Mary Magdalene. For whatever reason, Mary often gets a bum rap. Whether it is the false portrayal of her as more sinful than most or even as one of the prostitutes in the New Testament or in *The Da Vinci Code*, Mary gets a bum rap. But I want to suggest that Mary Magdalene might be the quintessential example of what it means to follow Jesus, to be his disciple, to be a person of the Way.

That's because Mary Magdalene was crazy. She shows up when she's not supposed to. She speaks up when others shut up. She stands up when everybody else sits down. She was crazy. Mary was somebody who obviously heard a different drummer. And folk like that are what the world calls crazy.

Think back to the crucifixion of Jesus. Crucifixion was

execution by the Empire for crimes against the state. It was public torture. It was an intentionally brutal means of capital punishment, an execution designed to send a message that revolution and revolutionaries would not be tolerated. If you were a supporter or follower of the person being crucified, it was dangerous to stand too close by during the execution. The rational and sensible thing to do was to go into hiding or even exile.

Having said that, let's call the roll of those Jesus asked to follow him, let's take the attendance of the apostles at the crucifixion of their Lord. Simon Peter? Absent. James? Absent. Andrew? Absent. Bartholomew? Absent. Judas? Absent. Mary Magdalene? Present and accounted for! When the old slaves sang, "Were you there when they crucified my Lord?," there was a woman named Mary who could answer, "I was there!" Now that's crazy!

But that's not all. On that Easter morning, who gets up and goes to the tomb of Jesus? Not Peter. Not Andrew. Not James. Not John. But Mary and some of the sisters! And it didn't make any sense. As I said, it was dangerous to be so closely associated with a person executed by the Empire. Going to the tomb made absolutely no sense. It's just plain crazy. The gospels say there was a large stone rolled in front of the tomb. Presumably Mary knew about it. She had no plan and no way to move that stone. But she went to the grave anyway. That's crazy. Matthew's gospel says the Romans had placed guards at the tomb. Mary had no plan and no way to take them out. But she got up and went anyway. That's crazy. And that craziness led to her being the first witness to the resurrection of Jesus from the dead, the first witness to the fact that the love of God is greater than any hatred humans can inflict. Because Mary was crazy like Christ, she was Christ's witness to the world. Brothers and sisters, Mary

Magdalene has shown us the way. She has shown us what we need. And what we need are some crazy Christians.

Now it may not be obvious at first, but we actually have a day to remember crazy Christians. I think we call it All Saints' Day. It's not called "All the Same Day," it's called All Saints' Day, because the saints, though they were fallible and mortal and sinners like the rest of us, when push came to shove they marched to the beat of a different drummer. In their lifetimes, they made a difference for the kingdom of God. As you know, we even have a book to help us commemorate them with prayers and readings and liturgy. We call it *Holy Women, Holy Men: Celebrating the Saints*. But we might as well call it *The Chronicles of Crazy Christians*.

One of the people we celebrate in the book is Harriet Beecher Stowe, a woman who used her words to set the captive free. She was born in 1811 into a devout family committed to the gospel of Jesus and to helping transform the world from the nightmare it often is into the dream God intends it to be. Beecher Stowe is best known for a novel titled *Uncle Tom's Cabin*. In this fiction, she told the truth. She told the story of how chattel slavery afflicted a family— afflicted real people. She told the truth of the brutality, the injustice, the inhumanity of the institution of chattel slavery. Her book did what YouTube videos of injustices and brutalities do today. It went nineteenth-century viral. It rallied abolitionists and enraged vested interests. The influence of that book was so powerful that Abraham Lincoln is reputed to have said, upon meeting Harriet Beecher Stowe for the first time, "So this is the little lady who started this great war!"[2]

In 1944, Beecher Stowe's witness was celebrated in a

---

2  *Holy Women, Holy Men: Celebrating the Saints* (New York: Church Publishing, 2010), 448.

Broadway play titled *Harriet* and dedicated to the work of
Eleanor Roosevelt. Helen Hayes played the part of Harriet
Beecher Stowe. At the end of the play Beecher Stowe's family
stands around her and sings the words of "The Battle Hymn
of the Republic," affirming the Christian witness of this
brave and bold woman. Part of the hymn goes like this:[3]

> *In the beauty of the lilies, Christ was born*
> *across the sea,*
> *With a glory in his bosom, that transfigured*
> *you and me:*
> *As he died to make men holy, let us die to*
> *make men free,*
> *While God is marching on.*
>
> *Glory, glory hallelujah,*
> *Glory, glory hallelujah,*
> *Glory, glory hallelujah,*
> *God's truth is marching on.*[4]

Beecher Stowe once explained her anti-slavery writing in
these words: "I wrote what I did because as a woman, as
a mother, I was oppressed and broken-hearted with the
sorrow and injustice I saw; because as a Christian I felt the
dishonor to Christianity; because as a lover of my country, I
trembled at the coming day of wrath."[5]

There's no doubt about it: Harriet Beecher Stowe was
crazy. A woman of her era was supposed to write nice
stories, not stories that would disturb the conscience of

3   Susan Belasco, "Harriet Beecher Stowe in Our Time," http://www.
    nationalera.wordpress.com
4   *Lift Every Voice and Sing II* (New York: Church Publishing, 1993), #226.
5   http://www.harrietbeecherstowecenter.org/hbs

a nation. A woman of her social standing was supposed to marry well, raise well-bred children, participate in a few charitable activities, and at her funeral be fondly remembered by all who knew her. That was the life she was supposed to have. But Beecher Stowe had been raised in a family that believed that following Jesus means changing the world from the nightmare it often is into the dream that God intends. And sometimes that means marching to the beat of a different drummer. Sometimes that means caring more when we are tempted to care less. Sometimes that means standing up when others are sitting down. Sometimes that means speaking up when others are shutting up. Sometimes that means being different. Sometimes that even means following Jesus, and being crazy.

After the death of Steve Jobs, one of the founders of Apple Inc., an old Apple Inc. commercial from the 1990s went viral on YouTube. It was a commercial whose goal had been to rebrand Apple products. The tag line for the commercial and for the company was: *Think different.*

In the commercial they showed a collage of photographs and film footage of people who have invented and inspired, created and sacrificed to improve the world, to make a difference. They showed Bob Dylan, Amelia Earhart, Frank Lloyd Wright, Maria Callas, Muhammad Ali, Martin Luther King Jr., Jim Henson, Mother Teresa, Albert Einstein, Pablo Casals, Mahatma Gandhi, Albert Schweitzer, and on and on and on. As the images rolled by, a voice read this poem:

> *Here's to the crazy ones. The misfits. The*
> *  rebels.*
> *The troublemakers. The round pegs in the*
> *  square holes.*

*The ones who see things differently. They're not
   fond of rules.*
*And they have no respect for the status quo.*
*You can quote them, disagree with them,
   glorify or vilify them.*
*About the only thing you can't do is ignore
   them.*
*Because they change things.*
*They invent. They imagine. They heal. They
   explore.*
*They create. They inspire. They push the
   human race forward.*
*Maybe they have to be crazy.*
*How else can you stare at an empty canvas
   and see a work of art?*
*Or sit in silence and hear a song that's never
   been written?*
*Or gaze at a red planet and see a laboratory
   on wheels?*
*While some see them as the crazy ones, we see
   genius.*
*Because the people who are crazy enough to
   think*
*they can change the world,*
*are the ones who do.*[6]

We could paraphrase that to say, the Christians who are crazy enough to think they can change the world are the ones who do. My friends, we need some of those crazy Christians. Sane, sanitized Christianity is killing us. Comfortable, demure Christianity may have worked once upon a time,

---

6  Apple's "Think Different" commercial, 1997.

but it won't carry the gospel anymore. We need some crazy Christians like Mary Magdalene and Harriet Beecher Stowe. Christians crazy enough to believe that God is real and that Jesus lives. Crazy enough to follow the radical way of the gospel. Crazy enough to believe that the love of God is greater than all the powers of evil and death. Crazy enough to believe, as Martin Luther King Jr. often said, "The arc of the moral universe is long, but it bends toward justice."[7] We need some Christians crazy enough to believe that children don't have to go to bed hungry; that the world doesn't have to be the way it often seems to be; that there is a way to lay down our swords and shields, down by the riverside; that as the slaves used to sing, "There's plenty good room in my Father's kingdom" because every human being in this world has been created in the image of God, and we are all equally children of God and meant to be treated as such.

What we need are some crazy Christians—Christians who are crazy enough to catch a glimpse of the crazy, transforming, transfiguring, life-changing vision of our Lord and Savior Jesus Christ. Christians who are crazy enough to follow him into the work of helping God to realize God's dream for all people and for all creation.

---

7    Taylor Branch, *Parting the Waters: America in the King Years 1954–63* (New York: Simon and Schuster, 1988), 197. The original quote is from the nineteenth-century abolitionist preacher Theodore Parker, who wrote that "the arc [of the moral universe] is a long one . . . And from what I see I am sure it bends toward justice." Theodore Parker, in *Ten Sermons of Religion* (Boston: Crosby, Nichols, & Co., 1853).

## CHAPTER TWO

# We Are Part of Something Greater Than Ourselves

"Go therefore and make disciples of all nations, baptizing them in the name of the Father and of the Son and of the Holy Spirit, and teaching them to obey everything that I have commanded you. And remember, I am with you always, to the end of the age." (Matthew 28:19–20)

God has a terrible habit of asking the impossible of people. If you don't believe me, ask Noah, or Abraham and Sarah, or David about to fight Goliath, or Queen Esther before the king, or Mary with her baby. This text, which we call the Great Commission, is a classic example. "Go therefore and make disciples of all nations." The words in the old King James Version said, "Go ye therefore and teach all nations. . . ." In the longer ending of Mark's gospel, Jesus says, "Go into all the world and proclaim the good news to the whole creation" (Mark 16:15). In the Acts of the Apostles, Jesus adds that the disciples "will be my witnesses in Jerusalem, in all Judea and Samaria, and to the ends of the earth" (Acts 1:8).

But think about that. How were the disciples supposed to go into all the world? They didn't even know where all the world was. None of the original disciples had ever traveled outside Palestine. They didn't know about most of the world existing. Marco Polo hadn't been to Asia. Columbus hadn't traveled west. Galileo had not been born. Alan Shepard hadn't traveled into outer space. Go into all the world?

Not only that, but how and with what were the disciples to go into all the world? Jesus gave them the task, but he didn't give them an organization to support them, he didn't provide any funding, and he didn't tell them how to set themselves up—no annual meeting, no diocesan convention, no General Convention, no Lambeth Conference. They had no smart phones, no fax machines, no email, no internet. Jesus didn't give them anything except a word and a promise.

Those disciples must have been getting anxious. Jesus asked them to do the impossible. "Go therefore and make disciples of all nations. . . ." But then look at what Jesus told them next: "And remember, I am with you always." That's the exact same thing God said to Moses when God told Moses to do the impossible. As the old spiritual goes, "Go down, Moses, way down in Egypt's land; tell old Pharaoh to let my people go."[1]

---

1  *Lift Every Voice and Sing II* (New York: Church Publishing, 1993), #228.

If you remember that story, Moses said something like, "Lord, are you crazy? Do you know who Pharaoh is? That's impossible!" But what did God say back to Moses? Just five words, but they were simple and they were clear: "I will be with you" (Exodus 3:12).

"I will be with you." In other words, do not fear, Moses, do not fear, disciples. Do not fear, because God is with you. And because you are part of something greater than yourselves, you will be able to do more than you ever could do on your own. You might even be able to do the impossible.

As Christians, we must live our lives against the backdrop of that which is greater than ourselves. Otherwise we'll spend our lives mired down in the constant micromanagement of a mess. But when we live our lives in the greater context of God and God's constant presence, things not only become manageable, they become transformed. Mountains you thought so incredibly high are not quite so high, and valleys you thought so low are not quite so low. Jesus understood this. And that is why he was able to summon the first disciples to do something of which they were thoroughly, utterly incapable.

People who have struggled against life's odds learn this wisdom quickly. If we live only in the context of the way things are, we are condemned to live according to the vagaries of the present time and the dictates of the status quo. But if we live in the context of that which is greater than ourselves, we become open to the possibility of action and transformation.

This may be the deeper meaning behind what Mary and Joseph did with the infant Jesus a month after he was born. Following ancient custom, they took the child to the Temple to be presented to the Lord. In presenting Jesus, they defined his life not against the backdrop of the first-century Roman

occupation of Palestine, but against the backdrop of his
Jewish history, his true ancestral identity, and the ultimate
reality of his being part of the people of God. In so doing
Mary and Joseph transformed their condition from "the
wretched of the earth," to borrow the phrase by the phi-
losopher Frantz Fanon, to the blessed and chosen of God.[2]
Their act proclaimed that their lives were part of something
greater than themselves.

Let's look a little deeper into this context God gives
us. The First Letter of John says, "[T]he one who is in you
is greater than the one who is in the world" (1 John 4:4).
Anselm of Canterbury wrote that God is that of which
nothing greater can be thought. The Rt. Rev. Barbara Harris,
the first woman to be consecrated a bishop in the Anglican
Communion, and one well acquainted with the struggle
and pain of progress, often says, "The God behind you is
greater than any problem ahead of you." Jesus tells us, "Go
therefore and make disciples of all nations." We can be part
of that impossible-sounding mission, especially and only
because we are part of something greater than ourselves.

When my siblings and I were little children, my father
sat us down one evening to talk. We knew something was
up. My father and other clergy had led some local efforts for
civil rights. That night, Daddy told us he might have to go
to jail the next day because he was going to be part of a protest. Then he told us something I still remember: "You must
always be willing to give yourself for a higher cause. Our
lives are part of something greater than ourselves."

A few years later my mother lapsed into a coma after an
aneurysm caused by a childhood head injury. For nearly a
year she was in the coma and eventually was moved from

---

2  Frantz Fanon, *The Wretched of the Earth* (New York: Grove Press, 2005).

the hospital to a nursing home. But that didn't mean we felt disconnected from her. Our family would spend part of every evening in the nursing home with Mommy. We did our homework there. We watched television there. We did family there, with her in a coma. Before we left we always prayed. Daddy's prayers were usually pretty short. Grandma, though, liked to "have a little talk with Jesus," as the hymn says—but in her case, 'little' didn't mean short in duration.[3]

Looking back now, I see how my family gave me some deep messages about life. Life can be tough. It's not always easy. But a life lived in the context of God can be a life triumphant, even when you're up against significant odds. When Mommy died sometime later, I remember thinking about what Daddy had said about a "higher cause" and that we are part of something greater than ourselves. And that made a difference. Life lived in the context of real faith in God is life that can be lived not according to the vicissitudes of life, but according to a hope in the ultimate victory of God.

Jesus sent the first disciples out on a mission that was clearly impossible. And by the power of an amazing grace and a sweet, sweet Spirit, they obeyed their Lord and began to fulfill his directions. I believe the same mission that Jesus gave the disciples is still the mission of our Church today. It excites me. It energizes me. And it scares me to death.

Even so, as that old hymn of Zion says, "It is no secret what God can do. What he's done for others, he'll do for you."[4] So go, sisters and brothers. Make disciples of all nations. And be not afraid. Our God is able, as Dr. King

---

3  *Lift Every Voice and Sing II* (New York: Church Publishing, 1993), #83.
4  http://www.gospelsonglyrics.org, by Stuart Hamblen.

once said, "to hew out of the mountain of despair a stone of hope."[5] Our God is able to make a way out of no way. From our caring and life-giving God, we know this truth: We are part of something greater than ourselves. And in fact, as Jesus calls us to follow him as our Savior and Lord, we may find we can even do what Christians have done for centuries before us—the impossible.

---

5   Martin Luther King Jr., "I Have a Dream" speech, August 28, 1963.

## CHAPTER THREE

# Following Jesus
# with Our Feet

For to this you have been called, because
Christ also suffered for you, leaving you an
example, so that you should follow in his
steps. (1 Peter 2:21)

A few days before I was consecrated bishop of the
Episcopal Diocese of North Carolina in June 2000, a group
of pilgrims left Holy Trinity Church in Greensboro, North
Carolina, to walk almost 60 miles to Duke Chapel in
Durham, North Carolina. They walked the highways and
the back roads in prayer and reflection and witness as the
diocese prepared to welcome me as their bishop. Little did
I realize at the time that their spiritual pilgrimage would
prove to be a parable of who we are as disciples of the Lord
Jesus Christ.

As they walked, they walked in the steps of Chaucer's Canterbury pilgrims. They walked in the tradition of John Bunyan's character Pilgrim in *The Pilgrim's Progress*. They walked in the steps of Mahatma Gandhi's Salt March to the Indian Ocean. They walked in the steps of those who marched across Selma's Edmund Pettis Bridge in 1965. Above all, they walked in the steps of Jesus of Nazareth, who summons disciples of every generation with the words, "Follow me." Their pilgrimage was part of other pilgrimages of the past, because in their walking they showed that discipleship is really about what you do with your feet.

The word 'disciple' in both Hebrew and Greek originates in education. A rabbi in ancient times, as in modern times, was not merely a teacher of the head but also a teacher of the heart. The rabbi taught a way of life. A pupil therefore was not simply an academic student. The pupil was a disciple who sought to live the way of and follow in the steps of the teacher.

Jesus reflected this understanding when he said: "A disciple is not above the teacher, nor a slave above the master; it is enough for the disciple to be like the teacher, and the slave like the master" (Matthew 10:24–25). He went on to say: "Follow me" (Mark 1:17), for "I am the way, and the truth, and the life" (John 14:6). This is the context in which Peter writes that those who would be Jesus' disciples "should follow in his steps" (1 Peter 2:21). Discipleship is about feet.

Frederick Buechner in his book *The Alphabet of Grace* includes this wonderful passage: "Feet are religious too. I say if you want to know who you are . . . you could do a lot worse than look at your feet for an answer. When you wake up in the morning, called by God to be a self again, if you want to know who you are, watch your feet. Because where your feet take you, that is who you are."[1]

Discipleship is not simply a theoretical concept. Discipleship is about feet. It is about discovering and claiming your true identity, because "where your feet take you, that is who you are."

Years ago I was asked to prepare two young men for Holy Baptism. Their mother, a Chinese Christian, had been associated as a girl with a mission to China founded by the Community of the Transfiguration, a religious order of the Episcopal Church based in Glendale, Ohio. Their mother had been imprisoned when the Chinese Communists took power, expelled Christian missionaries like the Transfiguration sisters, and imprisoned Christians like her. This remarkable woman of faith served nearly fifteen years in a Chinese prison, separated from her children, for refusing to bow to the Communist party line or to renounce her faith in Jesus Christ as Savior and Lord.

In the mid-1980s she was allowed to travel to the United States and reunite with the Episcopal Church. After a time, her sons were able to join her. Because she had been in prison, though, she had been unable to share her Christian faith with her young sons. I was asked to prepare them for baptism and confirmation.

When I met with the sons, I told them they were named for two of the very first disciples of Jesus. They looked at me quizzically and asked, "What's a disciple?" For a moment I was stumped. Then it dawned on me. I said to them, "Look at your mother. She followed Jesus even when it got her into trouble. That's a disciple."

---

1   Frederick Buechner, *The Alphabet of Grace* (New York/San Francisco: Harper & Row, 1970), 24–25.

When I said that, they got it. They got the idea that discipleship is about a life lived in love and liberating obedience to Jesus Christ. Discipleship is about following Jesus not only with your heart and your mind, but with your feet.

So it is not an accident that God tells Moses, "Remove the sandals from your feet, for the place on which you are standing is holy ground." And only after redirecting Moses' feet (Exodus 3:5), if you will, does God tell Moses, "I will send you to Pharaoh to bring my people, the Israelites, out of Egypt" (Exodus 3:10). It is not an accident that St. Paul, quoting Isaiah, uses the metaphor of feet for the very movement of the gospel: "How beautiful are the feet of those who bring good news" (Romans 10:15). Discipleship is about what you do with your feet, because discipleship is about following Jesus Christ as Lord and loving him as Savior.

The old hymn goes, "Where He leads me I will follow."[2] Discipleship is intrinsically holistic. It is about following Jesus with your feet, but also with your entire self. Do you remember the story of Jesus washing the feet of the disciples? It happened at the Last Supper as told by John's gospel. Jesus asks Peter to allow him to wash Peter's feet. Peter doesn't want Jesus to do it, but Jesus insists. Peter finally says okay, but then blurts out, "Lord, not my feet only but also my hands and my head!" (John 13:9). Peter, who sometimes didn't get what Jesus was trying to do, got it this time. To follow Jesus is to follow with the whole self—head, hands, and feet.

I'd like to take one last step. Discipleship, as Jesus articulates it, is universal. I believe that when Jesus said,

---

2  *Lift Every Voice and Sing II* (New York: Church Publishing, 1993), #144.

"Go therefore and make disciples of all nations," he meant what he said—*all* nations! We divide ourselves into various camps—evangelicals over here, social action folk over there; theological liberals here and conservatives there; high church, low church, broad church; people who want the pastoral church here, people who prefer the prophetic church there. But it seems to me that true discipleship moves us beyond these divisions, because discipleship is about following not ourselves, but Jesus. As Paul said: "[W]e do not proclaim ourselves; we proclaim Jesus Christ as Lord" (2 Corinthians 4:5).

The Church of England once sent a missionary priest to Africa to pastor and evangelize in a rural township. While there, the missionary met a young boy who became his most faithful acolyte. At one point the boy became ill and had to be hospitalized. Unfortunately, because of the poverty and politics of the land, the nearest hospital was some distance away. But during the child's illness, the priest visited him regularly and told him stories from the Bible, stories of Moses and Miriam and the Exodus, of David and Goliath, of Mary and her baby.

Eventually the boy recovered and came home. The church reassigned the priest, but he and the boy stayed in touch. In fact, the boy later went on to become ordained. The name of the missionary was Trevor Huddleston. The name of the boy was Desmond Tutu.[3] Now I wonder: Was that experience about evangelism, or social action? Was it liberal, or conservative? Was it high church, or low church? Was it pastoral, or prophetic? It didn't matter, of

---

3   Desmond Tutu, *Hope and Suffering* (Grand Rapids, MI: William B. Eerdmans Publishing Co., 1985), 9.

course. Trevor Huddleston and Desmond Tutu were simply following Jesus.

For the same Jesus who said, "You shall love the Lord your God" also quoted Moses to say, "You shall love your neighbor as yourself. On these two commandments hang all the law and the prophets" (Matthew 22:37–40). The same Jesus who said, "Go therefore and make disciples of all nations" also proclaimed the Year of Jubilee: "The Spirit of the Lord is upon me, because he has anointed me to proclaim good news to the poor. He has sent me to proclaim release to the captives and recovery of sight to the blind, to let the oppressed go free, to proclaim the year of the Lord's favor" (Luke 4:18–19). The same Jesus who is the Good Shepherd also cast the money changers out of the Temple. We don't have an evangelical or a social-ministry Jesus. We don't have a liberal or a conservative Jesus. We don't have a pastoral or a prophetic Jesus. We don't even have a high-church or a low-church Jesus, if we Episcopalians can believe that. I'm taking the Incarnation seriously here. We have *one* Lord Jesus Christ, truly God and truly human. And discipleship is about following that Jesus, our Lord and Savior.

While at General Convention in 2000, I was appointed to serve on the legislative committee on evangelism. This committee drafted the resolution "20/20: A Clear Vision," which calls for the Episcopal Church to double its size by the year 2020. Writing the resolution was certainly important, but for me the most profound memory I have was what happened among the committee members ourselves. Our group was a rather remarkable assembly of people— black and white, Anglo and Hispanic, Snow Belt and Sun Belt, gay and straight, liberal and traditional.

I am not suggesting everyone in that room agreed on

many concerns and issues. But I believe we did discover the deep source of our unity. We all shared something: a common commitment to follow Jesus Christ. And we shared a conviction and experience of the reality that God loves us, and that we love the Lord. Making disciples is about sharing that love and allowing others to know it and share it. Discipleship moves us beyond our usual personal and parochial and theological divisions to a new source of unity grounded in the gospel itself. As we follow Jesus' call, "Go and therefore make disciples of all nations," we are propelled by the grace of that unity.

We now have an opportunity to grow the Episcopal Church as a church for all peoples and nations and groups. The truth is, we are family. The Bible says, "From one ancestor [God] made all nations to inhabit the whole earth" (Acts 17:26). So we are family! We are sisters and brothers, one of another. The Rt. Rev. James Tengetenga is a dear friend who is Bishop of Southern Malawi and Chair of the Anglican Consultative Council. James likes to remind me that "in baptism, Jesus has made us family." He's right. St. Paul put it this way: "As many of you as were baptized into Christ have clothed yourselves with Christ. There is no longer Jew or Greek, there is no longer slave or free, there is no longer male and female; for all of you are one in Christ Jesus" (Galatians 3:27–28). I am convinced that God came among us in the person of Jesus to open the way and to show us the way to become more than merely an aggregation of individual self-interests, more than simply the human race or the human species. Jesus came to show us the way to become the human family of God.

We can do it, not simply to add numbers on the church rolls, but for the sake of the kingdom and in obedience to our Lord. And if we in the Church can become the human family of God, sisters and brothers together, then maybe we can bring that sense of sisterhood and brotherhood, the sense that we are all family, out into the world. Martin Luther King Jr. and a host of other people have said it: "We may have come here on different ships, but we're all in the same boat now."

I mentioned using our feet as a metaphor for discipleship. But I would like to add to that: Discipleship is also about hands. We are, as St. Paul taught us, the Body of Christ. If you shake someone else's hand and then shake your own hands, you'll see it's far easier to shake your neighbor's hand than it is to shake your own. I would daresay that is because we were made for each other. We were made to support each other and hold each other up. We'll walk together best when we join hands and do it together.

We need each other. We can do far more together than we can do apart or on our own. Large churches need small churches, and small churches need large churches. Small towns and rural areas need large cities, and vice versa. New churches need established churches. Our institutions need our congregations. Liberals need conservatives. Rich, poor, old, young, M.D., Ph.D., and no degree need each other. We are all part of an interconnected whole. We need each other. And we all need Jesus.

The truth is, as we follow Jesus with our feet, with our hands, with all "our selves, our souls and bodies,"[4] as we come to know Jesus' call to us and Jesus' love for us, we will discover the reality that we are each other's sisters and brothers in Christ and, together, heirs to God's eternal kingdom.

---

4  *The Book of Common Prayer* (New York: Church Hymnal Corp., 1986), 336.

As the great hymn says:

> In Christ there is no East or West,
> in him no South or North,
> but one great fellowship of love
> throughout the whole wide earth.

> Join hands, disciples of the faith,
> whate'er your race may be!
> Who serves my Father as his child
> is surely kin to me.

> In Christ now meet both East and West,
> in him meet South and North,
> all Christly souls are one in him,
> throughout the whole wide earth.[5]

---

5    *The Hymnal 1982* (New York: Church Hymnal Corp., 1985), #529.

## CHAPTER FOUR

# Living into God's Dream

> [Joseph's brothers] said to one another, "Here comes this dreamer. Come now, let us kill him and throw him into one of the pits; then we shall say that a wild animal has devoured him, and we shall see what will become of his dreams." (Genesis 37:19–20)

One of the delightful things about the families and households in the Bible is that they are so true to life. When you look below the surface, underneath the halos we have given them, these were real people. They were genuinely and marvelously human. The Bible doesn't cover up any of it, either. The biblical writers put it all out there, the good, the bad, and the disastrous. The characters' virtues ring true. Their vices ring even more true. The grace, the grits, the gravel, and the grandeur are all there. These folks were real.

And so is God—fully real. Through the good, the bad, and the many disasters, God worked with them and on them. Ultimately, in God's good and gracious time, God transformed their lives.

This was certainly true for the family of Jacob, Rachel, and Leah in which Joseph was one of many siblings. We who are parents know we aren't supposed to have a favorite child. That's not just a modern notion; biblical people knew that, too. They didn't need the psychologist Erik Erikson, the pediatrician Dr. Benjamin Spock, or the TV talk show host Oprah Winfrey to tell them that. And yet the Bible says Jacob "loved Joseph more than any other of his children" (Genesis 37:3).

This love inspired Jacob to give Joseph a special robe, the proverbial "coat of many colors" we learned about in Sunday School. The New Revised Standard Version of the Bible calls it "a long robe with sleeves." Some Bible translations and rabbinic commentaries call it an "ornamented tunic," a garment to be worn by royalty or people who were members of the leisure class.

Because of his privileged status, Joseph had time and opportunity to dream. While his brothers were out working hard in the fields, Joseph was dreaming. While they were tending the flocks in the heat of the Palestinian sun, Joseph was dreaming. While they were defending their family, the herds, and the flocks from predators and other dangers, Joseph was dreaming. While they were doing all the work, Joseph was sashaying around, tooting his own horn, taunting his brothers, and dreaming.

It wouldn't surprise anyone to learn that sibling rivalry reared its head. The other brothers formed a conspiracy. At a key point they said among themselves, "Here comes this dreamer. Come now, let us kill him and throw him into one of the pits; then we shall say that a wild animal has devoured him, and we shall see what will become of his dreams" (Genesis 37:19–20).

But as it turned out, they didn't kill Joseph. Another hand stayed their hands. Another plan was bigger than the brothers' plan. And another dream was bigger than the dreams of Joseph. The brothers sold Joseph to slave traders destined for Egypt (Genesis 37:26–28). As the story unfolds, the Hebrew writer reveals how Joseph the dreamer eventually saved his entire family from famine and death, and all because of his dream. At the end of the story we see an incredible moment of reconciliation between Joseph and his brothers, all because of the dream (Genesis 45). That's because Joseph's dreams were fragmentary parts of a larger dream—what Verna J. Dozier has called "the dream of God" for the human family and all creation.[1]

One night when I was ten years old, a group of ministers and community leaders met in our living room. I always liked to be near the action, so I was hanging around as the elders talked. At the time I didn't know what they were discussing, but it was clear they were working out the logistics of something important. It turned out they were planning to board a bus to Washington for a gathering that had been called for August—the 1963 March on Washington. I imagine that at the time, as they worked on details, looked for funding, settled conflicts among themselves, and organized a movement, they probably didn't realize they were part of a greater dream.

At the march, Dr. Martin Luther King Jr. gave voice to

---

1   Verna J. Dozier, *The Dream of God: A Call to Return* (Boston: Cowley, 1991).

what he called the dream of a new America, where there is liberty and justice for all. He proclaimed that this dream was "deeply rooted in the American dream that one day this nation will rise up and live out the true meaning of its creed—we hold these truths to be self-evident, that all men are created equal."[2]

The truth is, this dream of which King spoke is deeper than the American dream. It is as deep and as old as Sir Thomas More's concept of utopia, or Dante's vision of the transforming love of God. It is as deep and as old as Francis of Assisi giving up all that he had to proclaim good news to the poor. It is as deep and as old as John on the Isle of Patmos beholding a new heaven and a new earth where there is no more suffering and hardship and war (Revelation 21:1–4). It is as deep and as old as the apostle Paul declaring that in Christ there is neither Jew nor Greek, slave nor free, male nor female, but a new human family (Galatians 3:28). It is as deep and as old as the summons of the Great Commission to make disciples of all nations, building bridges, breaking boundaries, establishing the reign of God's kingdom (Matthew 28:19–20).

This dream is as deep and as old as Jesus at the Jordan and as that voice crying in the wilderness, "Repent, for the kingdom of heaven has come near" (Matthew 3:2). It is as deep and as old as the prophet Isaiah's messianic vision in which the wolf "shall live with the lamb" and in which people will no longer "hurt or destroy on all my holy mountain; for the earth will be full of the knowledge of the Lord as the waters cover the sea" (Isaiah 11:6, 9). It is as deep and as old as Moses, standing before Pharaoh and declaring,

---

2   James M. Washington, ed., *A Testament of Hope: Essential Writings of Martin Luther King Jr.* (San Francisco: Harper & Row, 1986).

"Thus says the Lord, the God of the Hebrews: Let my people go" (Exodus 9:1).

Ultimately this dream is as deep and as old as the dawn of creation, when "the morning stars sang together and all the angels shouted for joy" (Job 38:7). It is as deep and as old as when God, from the infinite depth of unbounded love, declared a beginning, "Let there be," and there was (Genesis 1:3). There is a dream!

The dream of God is a way of speaking of God's passionate love which seeks reconciliation, reunion, and communion between God and all of God's children. King said, "The cross is the eternal expression of the length to which God will go in order to restore broken community. The resurrection is a symbol of God's triumph over all forces that seek to block community. The Holy Spirit is the continuing community creating reality that moves through history."[3]

I'm coming to grips with the realization that God didn't create me because God needed me. That may not be news to you, but it was a moment of epiphany for me. God didn't create me because God needs me. In fact, if the truth be told, I'm one of God's biggest headaches. And I'll let you in on a secret—you're the other one. God didn't create us because God needed us. God created us because God loves us.

My Bible says that "God is love" (1 John 4:8). And love, as St. Paul taught us in 1 Corinthians 13, is not rude or boastful, love does not insist on its own way, love makes room and space for the other. It creates space for new possibilities and opportunities. God didn't create because of God's need, but out of God's love. We were created by love, for love, to love,

---

3  Martin Luther King Jr., *Stride Toward Freedom* (New York: Harper and Row, 1958), 105–106.

and to be loved. And we are at our best when we live in God's love, because that's what we were made for.

That is why our Lord Jesus Christ said, "'You shall love the Lord your God with all your heart, and with all your soul, and with all your mind.' This is the greatest and first commandment. And a second is like it: 'You shall love your neighbor as yourself.' On these two commandments hang all the law and the prophets" (Matthew 22:37–40). The key to life is to love God, to love each other, to love ourselves. The dream of God yearns toward realizing that community of love in which we are reconciled and in communion with our God, with each other, and with all creation.

A few years ago I received one of those computer-generated mailings that generously offered not only to research my family genealogy but also to sell me a copy of the Curry family crest. The advertisement read something like this: "Michael Curry, we have traced your ancestry to Ireland! You can now access your family seal, genealogy, and lots of information about your relatives!" I had to laugh. But who knows, someday I might have to take my family on a pilgrimage to my supposed ancestral home.

Still, I learned a truth from that mailing. At first glance, I chuckled that I didn't really have any relatives in Ireland. But then again, maybe I do. In God's eyes, maybe I do have some relatives over there. After all, I do believe we were created by one God—the one God who created and loves us all.

As the old song "There is a balm in Gilead" bids us sing:

> There is a balm in Gilead
> to make the wounded whole,
> there is a balm in Gilead,
> to heal the sin-sick soul.

If you cannot preach like Peter.
if you cannot pray like Paul,
you can tell the love of Jesus,
and say, "He died for all."[4]

Archbishop Desmond Tutu wrote, "God sent us here to help God realize God's dream of a new kind of society—gentle, caring, compassionate, sharing. 'When I am lifted up from the earth, [I] will draw all people to myself.' There are no outsiders or aliens. All, all are insiders. All belong. Black and white, rich and poor, young and old, male and female, educated, uneducated, gay, straight—all belong in this family of God, this human family, the Rainbow people of God. And God has no one but you to help God realize God's dream."[5]

As the Catechism in our prayer book states, "The mission of the Church is to restore all people to unity with God and each other in Christ."[6] St. Paul said that God "reconciled us to himself through Christ, and has given us the ministry of reconciliation" (2 Corinthians 5:18). God calls the Church to be a community of disciples committed to following Jesus Christ into God's dream for us and for all creation.

As we join together to worship God our Creator, it's about the dream. As we engage in evangelism and invite others to share this faith, it's about the dream. As we proclaim the gospel and reach out to serve others, it's about the dream. As we summon forth movements for justice and peace, it's about the dream. As we join with others to build a better world, it's about the dream—the dream of the love

---

4    *The Hymnal 1982* (New York: Church Hymnal Corp., 1985), #676.

5    Marcus Borg and Ross Mackenzie, eds., *God at 2000* (New York: Morehouse Publishing, 2000), 131. The quote is from John 12:32.

6    *The Book of Common Prayer* (New York: Church Hymnal Corp., 1986), 855.

of God ruling and transforming our lives and, in so doing, the life of the world.

It's no accident that Matthew's gospel sets the birth of Jesus in the context of dreams. The Joseph of Matthew, like the Joseph of Genesis, was a dreamer. When he learned that his fiancée, Mary, was pregnant and he was not the father, he wanted to break off the engagement. Many of us would call that reaction reasonable. Joseph's social construction of reality, maybe our social construction of reality, too, left no room for miracle. Then Joseph had a dream, and everything changed. The gospel tells us "an angel of the Lord appeared to him in a dream and said, 'Joseph, son of David, do not be afraid to take Mary as your wife, for the child conceived in her is from the Holy Spirit. She will bear a son, and you are to name him Jesus, for he will save his people from their sins'" (Matthew 1:20–21).

Joseph learned from his dream that the life in Mary's womb was the miracle of God's new possibility. In Jesus the dream of God, God's deepest intention, God's most profound purpose, God's greatest yearning, was to become flesh and dwell among us. The playwright George Bernard Shaw might as well have been speaking of the Joseph of Matthew when he wrote, "Some men see things as they are and ask why. Others dream things that never were and ask why not."[7]

We know our mission is to live God's dream by being the Body of Christ, disciples of the Lord Jesus Christ, who charges us so boldly and so lovingly to carry out God's dream. But the question is, how do we help make God's dream a reality? First we must affirm what God is already doing among us, especially as Christians in the Anglican

---

7 George Bernard Shaw, *Selected Plays with Prefaces, Volume 2* (New York: Dodd, Mead & Co., 1949), 7.

tradition. Herbert O'Driscoll writes that when we share the good news of Jesus with others, we need to share that good news as we have experienced it. O'Driscoll depicts Satan trying to trick unwary Christians—much like Screwtape, the wily senior demon in C. S. Lewis' *The Screwtape Letters*. These are the instructions that O'Driscoll's devil gives:

> Whatever you do, make certain that Anglicans judge themselves by criteria other than their own. Keep them asking why they cannot produce a succession of Billy Grahams, but never let them wonder why they possess the beauty of George Herbert's poetry, the insights of Evelyn Underhill's mysticism, the integrity of Kenneth Leech's spirituality, the brilliance of Sally McFague in linking Christian theology with environmental issues, the courage of Desmond Tutu in South Africa.[8]

To carry out God's dream, we also need to discern how the Holy Spirit is moving in the world, and to do that we need to set aside some time to pray. When my grandma would face an important and complex decision, she'd often say, "Let me pray on that." To pray on it as Grandma did was to ask God about it, to consider the question in the context of God's will. Only after she sensed God's path for her would she make a decision; then and only then would she act.

In addition, we need to be open to the Spirit prompting us to witness to a world hungry and yearning for the good news. Jesus was teaching us this when he said, "You are the

---

8  Herbert O'Driscoll, *Confound Them: Diabolical Plans for the Church* (Toronto: Anglican Book Centre, 2002), 57.

light of the world" and "let your light shine before others, so they may see your good works and give glory to your Father in heaven" (Matthew 5:14, 16). As Christopher Duraisingh of the Episcopal Divinity School in Cambridge, Massachusetts, wrote in an essay on today's Anglican Communion:

> The church cannot domesticate mission and manage it. It simply "gets-in-behind" the Spirit of God who is witnessing from within the world and within human hearts to the movement of the new creation that God incessantly brings about. . . . In dialogue with the Spirit, and in dialogue with all others who discern the movement of the Spirit in their own contexts and in their own way, Christians can get ready for witnessing to their own story.[9]

Soon after the September 11 terrorist attack, when airplanes began to take to the sky again, I had to fly to a meeting of the House of Bishops of the Episcopal Church. On my flight to New York I found myself sitting next to a man who looked Middle Eastern. I don't believe in profiling, but I must be honest; I hesitated to sit next to him. I wondered, "Could this guy be a terrorist?" As it turned out, he was an American of Pakistani background, actually a physician on his way to a medical conference. We struck up a conversation. Eventually we exchanged photos of our families. I kept feeling guilty for having judged him simply by his appearance.

---

9   Christopher Duraisingh, "Toward a Postcolonial Re-visioning of the Church's Faith, Witness, and Communion," in *Beyond Colonial Anglicanism: The Anglican Communion in the Twenty-First Century,* Ian T. Douglas and Kwok Pui-lan, eds. (New York: Church Publishing, 2001), 354–355.

At one point in our conversation he asked me to pray for him. Even though I was by then a bishop, I wasn't quite sure how to do that. I had prayed with Jews but never with a Muslim. Still, we decided to pray together from our different traditions. As we sat side by side, we had a prayer meeting at 20,000 feet—and oh, what a joy it was. We held hands and we prayed. And I knew God was there. Deep in my heart, I knew I was doing as Jesus would do. I was following my Lord.

As we prayed, I could see the dream—the dream of a world where the gospel of love is lived and is real. The dream of a world in which the bridges of love are built and the highways of justice are established. The dream of a world where there is no more hunger, no more war, no more poverty, no more suffering, no more harm. The dream of a humanity reconciled to God, to each other, and to all of creation.

We need to become dreamers, just like the Josephs of old. We need to rededicate ourselves to that dream and let the dream of God be our mission. Let us live that dream and "let justice roll down like waters, and righteousness like an ever-flowing stream" (Amos 5:24). Let us live that dream until every man and woman sits under his or her own vine and fig tree and lays down their swords and shields, down by the riverside, to study war no more (Micah 4:4; Isaiah 2:4). Let us live that dream until every valley is exalted, every mountain and hill made low. Let us live that dream until the crooked are made straight and the rough places become a plain. And as we do that, as we live into the dream of God, we can know that "the glory of the Lord shall be revealed, and all people shall see it together" (Isaiah 40:5).

## CHAPTER FIVE

# A Mountain Climb that Can Change the World

In days to come the mountain of the Lord's house shall be established as the highest of the mountains, and shall be raised above the hills; all the nations shall stream to it. Many peoples shall come and say: "Come, let us go up to the mountain of the Lord, to the house of the God of Jacob; that he may teach us his ways and that we may walk in his paths." For out of Zion shall go forth instruction, and the word of the Lord from Jerusalem. He shall judge between the nations, and shall arbitrate for many peoples; they shall beat their swords into plowshares, and their

> spears into pruning hooks; nation shall not
> lift up sword against nation, neither shall they
> learn war any more. (Isaiah 2:2–4)

Biblical writers described the heart and soul of their stories through the landscape of the biblical world. They gave us the Red Sea, the fleshpots of Egypt, the wilderness in which the children of Abraham wandered, the Valley of Jezreel, the hills and sea of Galilee, the River Jordan, the Dead Sea, the Promised Land, and the valley of the dry bones. They even created geographical images as they described the hoped-for future as that time when "[e]very valley shall be lifted up, and every mountain and hill be made low" (Isaiah 40:4). In the Bible, geography is theology.

In this light, mountains take on profound meaning in the Bible, especially in the writings of Isaiah. Mountains provide a way of talking about those places, moments, and ways in which human beings experience the presence and the transforming reality of God. Mountains are a means of talking about what the Celtic tradition calls "thin places," in which the temporal realm enters the infinite. Mountains represent those times when "God happens" for us and when that experience changes our world.

It was on the mountain called Moriah that Abraham nearly sacrificed his son Isaac because of what he heard God asking him to do. It was on that mountain that the angel stayed Abraham's hand until he learned that grace is closer to the heart of God than stern sacrifice and blind obedience (Genesis 22:1–19). It was on the mountain called Horeb, or Sinai, that Moses encountered God in a burning bush. Moses came to the mountain running from his past. He left the mountain on a mission of emancipation (Exodus 3:1–22). "Go down, Moses, way down in Egypt's land; tell old Pharaoh to let my people go."[1] Later on that mountain, God gave Moses the Ten Commandments that would change and revive the life of the people. The mountain is a place of transformation.

The writer of Isaiah envisions the mountain as the place where people will experience God's love and the reign of God's kingdom. On the mountaintop they "shall beat their swords into plowshares." On the mountaintop God will establish that peaceable kingdom where "the wolf shall live with the lamb." On the mountaintop they "will not hurt or destroy on all my holy mountain; for the earth will be full of the knowledge of the Lord as the waters cover the sea." And on the mountaintop Isaiah beholds the "new heavens and a new earth" (Isaiah 2:4; 11:6; 65:25; 11:9).

It is, therefore, not an accident that we have a Sermon on the Mount; or that Jesus designated the twelve apostles on a mountain; or that Jesus must climb the mount of Transfiguration before he can walk in the lonesome valley, bearing the cross. It is no coincidence that at the end of Matthew's gospel, Jesus gives the Great Commission and sends forth the disciples into the world to preach the gospel and make disciples—from a mountain (Matthew 5–7; Mark 3:13; Mark 9:2–8; Matthew 28:16–20). The mountain is the place of God's transforming, renewing, and reconciling presence. Come, let us go to the mountain of the Lord.

On the mountain, God transfigures the world from the nightmare of death and destruction into God's dream of Shalom and wholeness and life. At the heart of that worldwide transformation are men, women, and children whose lives are being changed. The biblical writer has moved from

---

1   *Lift Every Voice and Sing II* (New York: Church Publishing, 1993), #228.

a narrow focus solely on his own tribe to a vision of people from all nations and races and clans and kinds gathered around the mountain. He has seen a new humanity, a new creation. The writer understands that people transformed by their relationship with God and each other become agents in God's transformation of the world. Listen to the text again:

> "Come, let us go up to the mountain of the Lord, to the house of the God of Jacob; that he may teach us his ways and that we may walk in his paths." For out of Zion shall go forth instruction, and the word of the Lord from Jerusalem. He shall judge between the nations, and shall arbitrate for many peoples; they shall beat their swords into plowshares, and their spears into pruning hooks; nation shall not lift up sword against nation, neither shall they learn war any more. (Isaiah 2:3–4)

I notice a three-fold pattern of transformation in this text: People come. They learn. And they live differently. First, they come. On the mountain they enter a deeper relationship with God and with each other. In the sixth century a monk named Dorotheos of Gaza taught that the goal of the Christian life is to live within the love of God. He said creation is like the spokes of a wheel, with God as the center. The closer we come to the center of that wheel and to God, the closer we come to each other. And alternatively, the closer we draw to each other, the closer we come to God, for we are all children of God and we have all been created in God's image and likeness.[2] We come to the mountain,

---

2   Roberta Bondi, *To Love as God Loves: Conversations with the Early Church* (Philadelphia: Fortress Press, 1987), 25.

then, and experience a deepened and revived relationship with God and with each other.

Second, people learn. "Come, let us go up to the mountain of the Lord, to the house of the God of Jacob; that he may teach us his ways. . . . For out of Zion shall go forth instruction." They listen and learn Torah, God's message, God's instruction, God's teaching and word for life.

Third, people live differently. They walk in God's paths. They live God's ways of love and life. They "beat their swords into plowshares, and their spears into pruning hooks." They do not make war anymore, because they have learned God's ways. It's like the old hymn that says, "Goin' to lay down my sword and shield, Down by the riverside; To study war no more."[3] People come. They learn. They live differently. And in so doing, they are transformed and share in God's transformation of the world.

You will notice this three-fold pattern in how Jesus forms his disciples and sends them out. First he invites his disciples to come. "Come and see," he says, "Follow me" (John 1:39; Mark 1:17). Jesus beckons his disciples to him in order to enter into a deepened relationship, through him, with God and each other in community. That is what baptism is about, a deepened relationship with God and each other in Christ.

Second, Jesus teaches his disciples. They learn not just through his words but also from his actions and even his presence. They learn the good news: "Come to me, all you that are weary and are carrying heavy burdens, and I will give you rest. Take my yoke upon you, and learn from me; for I am gentle and humble in heart, and you will find rest

---

3   *Lift Every Voice and Sing II* (New York: Church Publishing, 1993), #210.

for your souls. For my yoke is easy, and my burden is light" (Matthew 11:28–30).

Jesus calls his first disciples in chapter four of Matthew's gospel; in the very next chapter, he takes them up a mountain to teach them in the Sermon on the Mount (Matthew 4:18–25 and Matthew chapters 5–7). Theologian William Countryman observed about the power of Jesus' teachings: "People in our own time often need to encounter Jesus first not in terms of a religion that sometimes falls egregiously short of its founder's standards, but in terms of a life-transforming message. Remember that Jesus' first hearers welcomed that message because it changed their lives and their worlds."[4]

If you look at the words of the Great Commission, you'll see this is precisely how Jesus forms his disciples. After the resurrection, Jesus takes the disciples to a mountain. He tells them: "Go therefore and make disciples of all nations, baptizing them in the name of the Father and of the Son and of the Holy Spirit, and teaching them to obey everything that I have commanded you" (Matthew 28:19–20). We form disciples through baptism and teaching so they might come into a deepened, transforming relationship with God and each other, as we learn and live the gospel of Jesus.

Third, this deepened relationship transforms us so that we live differently as the community of Jesus. But what does it mean to live differently? Let's look at the story of the Transfiguration in the ninth chapter of Mark's gospel. As Jesus approaches his death, he takes Peter, James, and John up a mountain. As they pray, the disciples behold Jesus transfigured and changed, as if they can see his very humanity illuminated by his very divinity.

---

4   http://www.thewitness.org/archive/oct2002/countryman.html

In the vision the disciples also see Moses and Elijah talking to Jesus. That is significant for several reasons, but let me focus here on one. The Old Testament tells us that both Moses and Elijah go to a mountain. They go to the mountain of God, are transformed by their encounter with God, and go forth from the mountain to live differently and change the world. Their spiritual transformation did not cause them to avoid the world; it led them to engage the world in a deeper way and to share in God's mission of repairing the world.

Therefore I do not think it an accident that Moses and Elijah are present as Jesus is transfigured on a mountain. And I do not think it an accident that, like the two prophets of old, Jesus leaves the Mount of the Transfiguration and goes into the world to take up the cross, to sacrifice himself, and to bring new life to the world.

I once served a congregation in Cincinnati founded by the Community of the Transfiguration, an Episcopal religious order in Glendale, Ohio. I'm still an associate of the community, and one spring at a retreat I was sitting in the chapel, which is dedicated to the Transfiguration of Jesus. A beautiful mural above the high altar depicts the Transfiguration of Jesus as told in the New Testament.

As I sat, I gazed at the mural. And something happened. Now I'm not really given to mystic visions. That's not in my spiritual gift set, as far as I know. But that day I imagined something I would call mystical. As I focused on the mural, I saw Jesus being transfigured and reshaped, not into something he wasn't, but into a disclosure of who he was and is. In my imagination his shape was altered, stretched, like an image in a Surrealist Salvador Dali painting. But it was not just Jesus being transfigured and stretched. The disciples Peter, James, and John were also being stretched—into the shape of Jesus. And the landscape of the world around them was being stretched, too—transformed and transfigured in the same way, in a new way.

It was as though I could see in that moment a world stretched and transfigured by the incredible love of God that we experience in Jesus, a world stretched and transfigured by the faith, the justice, the mercy, the compassion of God that we experience in Jesus. That stretching and transfiguration is, itself, the transforming journey of discipleship. That is what it means to be a disciple. That is what it means to make a difference in this world. That is what it means to live the dream of God.

At the foundation of all of this are God's words to God's people: "A new heart I will give you, and a new spirit I will put within you" (Ezekiel 36:26). God promises that "this is the covenant that I will make with the house of Israel. . . . I will put my law within them, and I will write it on their hearts; and I will be their God, and they shall be my people. No longer shall they teach one another, or say to each other, 'Know the Lord,' for they shall all know me, from the least of them to the greatest, says the Lord" (Jeremiah 31:33–34).

From a new heart comes a new life. An old hymn based on Psalm 51 goes, "Give me a clean heart so I may serve Thee."[5] Transformed hearts yield transformed lives. And transformed lives transform the world. I have an abiding conviction that the love of God that we know in the gospel of Jesus Christ is the world's most powerful source of transformation. I have an abiding conviction that the gospel of Jesus Christ can change our lives and the life of the world for the good.

---

5   *Lift Every Voice and Sing II* (New York: Church Publishing, 1993), #124.

I grew up in the Episcopal Church, born and bred. In this community of faith I came to know Jesus and God's love. But when I went off to college I did what many young people do. I was free from home, and I reveled in that freedom. Now, much of what I did as a student was pretty normal. But at one point I got close to the edge. Then one of my best friends nearly died from a drug overdose. Fortunately he did not die, but he came very close. I remember going back to my dorm room that night, confused and trying to sort it all out. I was sitting on the edge of my bed when my grandmother's face came to me.

Grandma was a remarkable woman of simple, strong, and profound faith. She lived through Jim Crow. She buried a husband and several children. She buried my mother who had died in her 40s, then Grandma turned around in her 70s and helped raise us. I knew deep down that the key to her life was her faith in Jesus Christ. She used to say, "We've got a good God and a good gospel." That night in college, Grandma's face came to me, and I got down on my knees and prayed. In the weeks that followed, I also had some talks with a kind and wise college chaplain who gently guided me along the way. And as time went by, I experienced an awakening. It was not that I had never known God. It was more that I became unquestioningly aware of what I had always known. I became genuinely conscious of what my family and my church had taught me. For me, it was a kind of coming home to knowing God again, to being a believer, but as if it were for the first time.

Jesus continues to transform my life. I know I am not his best disciple. I have my good side, but I'm also broken and sinful. But I'll quote the old gospel song that became the title of a book by Maya Angelou, because I "wouldn't take nothing for my journey now."[6] I love the Lord. And I pray that the gospel will continue to change my life.

"'Come, let us go up to the mountain of the Lord, to the house of the God of Jacob; that he may teach us his ways and that we may walk in his paths.' . . . [T]hey shall beat their swords into plowshares, and their spears into pruning hooks; nation shall not lift up sword against nation, neither shall they learn war any more." As the hymn says: "Walk together, children, don't you get weary, there's a great camp meeting in the Promised Land."[7] Discipleship happens as we come, as we learn, and as we live differently in the community of Jesus. We are transformed, and we gain the will and the inspiration to participate in God's transformation of the world. Ultimately we begin to live into God's call of making disciples, making a difference in the world, and bearing witness to Isaiah's bold vision of the "new heavens and a new earth." Jesus calls us all, every one of us, to come! To learn! To live differently! And to share in God's transformation of the world!

---

6   Maya Angelou, *Wouldn't Take Nothing for My Journey Now* (New York: Random House, 1993).

7   Negro Spiritual, http://www.negrospirituals.com

## CHAPTER SIX

# Down with Walls of Division and Up with the Dream of God

For he [Jesus] is our peace; in his flesh he has made both groups [Jews and Gentiles] into one and has broken down the dividing wall, that is, the hostility between us. He has abolished the law with its commandments and ordinances, that he might create in himself one new humanity in place of the two, thus making peace, and might reconcile both groups to God in one body through the cross, thus putting to death that hostility through it. So he came and proclaimed peace to you who were far off and peace to those who were near; for through him both

of us have access in one Spirit to the Father.
(Ephesians 2:14–18)

After the 2003 General Convention of the Episcopal Church voted to consent to the election of the Rev. Canon V. Gene Robinson as Bishop Coadjutor of the Diocese of New Hampshire, I found myself looking deep within. I started asking myself some penetrating questions about the God in whom I believe, about Jesus who is my Savior and Lord, and about the Church I love and of which I am a part. The controversy at that convention over the issue of sexuality had prompted me to wonder: What do I really believe, at the deepest levels, as a disciple of Jesus Christ? What do I really believe about the Church? And what do I believe about this world in which we live?

The passage above from the second chapter of the epistle to the Ephesians began to emerge as a guidepost for my reflections. I did a little research and discovered that "the dividing wall" it refers to might well have been a feature of the Jerusalem Temple. In those days the Temple was one of the world's architectural marvels. In addition to its beauty and liturgical efficiency, however, its design made a clear statement about the stratification of both religion and society. The Temple had separate worship areas that delineated where the religious authorities allowed certain categories of people to go.

An area called the Holy of Holies was considered the most sacred place in the Temple. Only the High Priest could enter there, and only to perform acts of repentance for the whole nation on the Day of Atonement. Fanning outward was a Court of the Priests where only priests were allowed, then a Court of Israel reserved for Jewish males. Still farther out lay the Court of Women with the women's gallery. And then came a wall that separated all of these areas from an outside area called the Court of the Gentiles.

I learned that in 1871 archeologists in Jerusalem came upon an inscription dating from the time of Jesus that minced no words in clarifying the purpose of the wall separating Jew from Gentile. The inscription warned Gentiles that "to cross this boundary in the temple is to risk death."[1]

This sociological reality of the dividing wall may well explain why Jesus cleansed the Temple just before he died with the words of the prophet Isaiah on his lips: "My house shall be called a house of prayer for all the nations" (Mark 11:17; see Isaiah 56:7).

In the epistle to the Ephesians, the writer sees the death of Jesus as an act of selfless love in which the reach of God's grace and the expanse of God's embrace have broken down barriers that divide us from God and from each other. By giving his life in this cause, by shedding his blood, Jesus has opened the way to a new life born of faith, not of law, in which he destroys walls that divide and establishes bridges that build a new creation of reconciliation, compassion, love, justice, and peace.

The writer of Ephesians sees this realization as the key to understanding God's continuing work in creation. In Jesus, God fully reveals the divine plan and purpose. That plan is "to gather up all things" in Christ (Ephesians 1:10). That plan is to reconcile all people to God and to

---

1 Walter Harrelson, *The New Interpreter's Study Bible* (Nashville, TN: Abingdon Press, 2003). See also Bruce M. Metzger and Michael David Coogan, *The Oxford Companion to the Bible* (New York: Oxford University Press USA, 1993), 733–734.

each other (Ephesians 2:16). Old Testament scholar Walter Brueggemann has written, "The central vision of world history in the Bible is that all of creation is one, every creature in community with every other, living in harmony and security toward the joy and well-being of every other creature."[2]

This perspective of unity amidst diversity enjoys a long and rich biblical history. If you survey the grand sweep of the biblical story, you can see this perspective unfolding until it reaches its fullest revelation in Jesus Christ. As the people of the Bible enter more deeply into God's purposes and plans, they continually encounter this pattern of God reaching out to others, gathering, embracing, inviting. As time goes by, they discover that the reach of God's grace and the extent of God's embrace to all people are more expansive than they could ever have imagined.

Let me suggest some Scriptural examples of this reaching out. Do you remember the story of Noah and the flood in chapters six through nine of Genesis? Noah builds an ark, probably thinking that his mission is to save his own neck. But as he actually lives into God's purpose and plan, he discovers that this ark-building is part of God's mission of building a renewed world. The Jewish tradition calls this activity of God *tikkun olam*—the repair, the rebuilding, the healing of creation. At the end of the story God gives Noah the rainbow sign: never again will God threaten to destroy the world by flood. God creates a covenant not just with Noah and his human descendants, but a covenant with all creation.

In Genesis 12, God calls Abram (later named Abraham) and Sarai (later named Sarah) from their homeland to go to

2   Walter Brueggemann, *Living Toward a Vision: Biblical Reflections on Shalom* (Cleveland: Pilgrim Press, 1982), 15–16.

a land they do not know. As the story develops, it becomes clear that Abraham and Sarah and their descendants understand God's promise to Abraham as primarily to the Jewish people. But if you look at the text of Genesis 12, you see that God's promise to Abraham and Sarah contains the ultimate goal that "in you all the families of the earth shall be blessed" (Genesis 12:3).

Consider the Exodus. The Hebrew people are slaves in Egypt. God sends Moses to liberate them. As far as we can tell, Moses thinks God's freedom movement concerns only the Hebrew slaves. But as the story unfolds, and as the Jewish and Christian traditions evolve, the Exodus to the Promised Land becomes the model for a wider, more universal vision of the freedom that God intends for all people and all creation.

Perhaps the most explicit example occurs in the book of Jonah. God tells Jonah to go preach to the Gentile people of Assyria. Jonah resists. He tries to run away. Instead of heading east to Assyria, he boards a boat and heads west toward Spain. You know the rest of the story. The storm. The great fish. And Jonah ends up in Assyria anyway. By the end of the story, Jonah has discovered that God's mercy and grace have no limits. The same grace that could reach him in the belly of the great fish could reach out to the people he considered his enemies.

Several years ago I went on pilgrimage to the Middle East. In Jerusalem we stayed at the guest house of St. George's, the Anglican cathedral. While walking in the cathedral close, I ran into one of the members of the staff. We struck up a conversation that lasted well over an hour. As we talked into the night, we shared stories. He was as interested in my story as I was in his. He asked how I became Christian. I told him about my family and background.

He told me he was a Palestinian and an Anglican. I asked him when he and his family became Christian. He answered, "On the day of Pentecost." He must have seen me do a double-take, because he went on to explain. "My people are those mentioned in the Old Testament as the Hittites and the Jebusites. We were cut off from knowing the promises of God. But Jesus came, and in his death he broke down the dividing wall that separated Jew from Gentile. On the day of Pentecost, the Spirit of Jesus made it possible for all people to hear the message of the gospel. My ancestors were actually there—in fact, they were mentioned in the story of Pentecost."

That same story of what some call the birth of the Church, the day of Pentecost, speaks of barriers being bridged and divisions being overcome. On Pentecost, people heard the gospel of Jesus. And as they heard the gospel, barriers came tumbling down, bridges arose, and the new humanity in Christ began to emerge.

In his sermon collection, Peter Storey—who was a Methodist Bishop in Johannesburg and Soweto—quotes from a book titled *Manna and Mercy: A Brief History of God's Unfolding Promise to Mend the Entire Universe*. The author, Daniel Erlander, spent some time combing through the gospels to make a list of the types of people Jesus encountered: lepers, prostitutes, tax collectors, sinners, poor people, discarded people, blind people, debtors, outcasts, children, women, men, elderly people, sick people, Gentiles, Samaritans, Jews, the demon-possessed, outsiders, heretics, Pharisees, lawyers, rich people. Erlander then made a list of the verbs the gospels used to describe how Jesus related to these people: "invited," "included," "affirmed," "loved," "touched," "liberated," "held," "embraced," "healed," "cleansed," "given dignity," "fed," "forgiven," "made whole," "called," "reborn," "given hope," "received," "honored," "freed."[3]

Bishop Storey concluded that this was the kind of new life that Jesus offered in his encounters. Jesus excluded no one. He held back nothing. He built bridges among people, and they gained new life. "That's what happened when Jesus was around," Storey wrote. "Not a single person excluded, not a single grace held back."[4] St. Paul wrote that "if anyone is in Christ, there is a new creation: everything old has passed away; see, everything has become new! All this is from God, who . . . has given us the ministry of reconciliation" (2 Corinthians 5:17–18).

Theologians tell us that the essence of sin is separation from God, from each other, and from creation. In contrast, Jesus' actions demonstrate engagement, involvement, connection, reconciliation. As Jesus' followers, we understand that the work of the gospel, the core of discipleship, is to follow our Savior in the way of God, breaking down dividing walls and divisive barriers and building up bridges of reconciliation that lead to a new humanity, a new creation, a new heaven, and a new earth.

The World Council of Churches once affirmed this purpose by stating, "The reconciliation brought about by the cross is the basis of the mission of the Church. A reconciled and renewed creation is the goal of the mission of the church. The vision of God uniting all things in Christ

---

3 Daniel Erlander, *Manna and Mercy: A Brief History of God's Unfolding Promise to Mend the Entire Universe* (Mercer Island, WA: The Order of Saints Martin and Teresa, 1992), 45.

4 Peter Storey, *With God in the Crucible: Preaching Costly Discipleship* (Nashville, TN: Abingdon Press, 2002), 165.

is the driving force of its life and sharing."[5] That is a call worthy of our claim and for which we can give our lives. That mission is ours.

This understanding of the Church's mission has long been part of our Anglican tradition. In the sixteenth century Queen Elizabeth I, in what has become known as the Elizabethan Settlement, shaped a united Church of England out of diverse and conflicted Protestant and Catholic factions. Richard Hooker, the great theologian of Elizabethan Anglicanism, reportedly said: "I pray that none will be offended if I seek to make the Christian Religion an inn where all are received joyously, rather than a cottage where some few friends or the family are to be received."[6]

I want to see the Episcopal Church embrace its mission as a Christian community in which the diversity among us is honored and respected. Some of that diversity reflects the rich tapestry of our various ethnic and racial backgrounds. Some of that diversity is found in our gender. Some of it includes differences of sexual orientation. Some of it is socio-economic. Some of it is linguistic and cultural. Some of it is political and ideological. Some is theological. We are all kinds and stripes, all sorts and conditions of our common humanity.

That variety is inherent in the Body of Christ if it is to reflect the work of God that breaks barriers and builds bridges. St. Paul says of this variety and diversity in the Body of Christ, "The eye cannot say to the hand, 'I have no need of you,' nor again the head to the feet, 'I have no need

---

5 The Canberra Assembly of the World Council of Churches, http://oikoumene.net/eng.canberra91/eng.canber.2.7/index.html

6 This quote is often attributed to sixteenth-century theologian Richard Hooker, although the source is uncertain.

of you.' . . . Now you are the Body of Christ and individually members of it" (1 Corinthians 12:21, 27). Such diversity can be challenging, though.

After the consecration of Bishop Gene Robinson, some stark differences among us emerged. We have had to be intentional about encouraging holy and respectful conversations as we wrestle with concerns where there are deep differences among us. We've worked at learning to listen to each other, pray for each other, love each other, and discern together what the Spirit might be saying to the Church.

As I have mentioned before, my parents grew up Baptist and became Episcopalians in their young adult years. My mother was confirmed while in graduate school after reading the works of C.S. Lewis. When my parents met, my mother was an Episcopalian. My father was in seminary and licensed as a Baptist preacher.

During their courtship my father one Sunday decided to attend church with my mother. He had never been inside an Episcopal church. It was an alien world to a person who came from the African-American Baptist tradition. *The Book of Common Prayer,* the liturgy, the written prayers, the silences, the chanting—all were new. But he later said the most striking difference for him that day was communion. He had never experienced a chalice, the common cup from which everyone drank. That morning my parents were among the few African-Americans in the congregation. This was the 1940s. Jim Crow was alive and well. Segregation and separation of the races was still the law in much of the land. The armed forces had not yet been integrated. *Brown v. the Board of Education* had not taken place, and it was long before the Montgomery bus boycott. Martin Luther King Jr. was still in seminary.

Still, my father saw on the altar only one cup from which everyone was to drink.

My father didn't feel comfortable going up for communion, but when my mother went up, he watched closely. Was the priest really going to give her communion from the common cup? And if he did, was the next person really going to drink from that same cup? And would others drink too, knowing a black woman had sipped from that cup? He saw the priest offer her the cup, and she drank. Then the priest offered the cup to the next person at the rail, and that person drank. And then the next person, and the next, all down the rail. When my father told the story, he would always say: "That's what brought me to the Episcopal Church. Any church in which black folks and white folks drink out of the same cup knows something about a gospel that I want to be a part of."

The gospel, the good news of God's reconciling love in Jesus Christ, can transform people and societies, despite their diversity, from the world's nightmare of division into God's intention for reconciliation. Luke's gospel frames this message in the story of who is included at Jesus' birth. Shepherds in the biblical world were not the pastoral characters we often see in Christmas cards or nativity plays. Raymond E. Brown in his book *The Birth of the Messiah* says of shepherds in the biblical world, "Far from being regarded as either gentle or noble, in Jesus' time shepherds were often considered dishonest, outside the Law." He also says that "herdsmen were added by the early rabbis to the list of those ineligible to be judges or witnesses since they frequently grazed their flocks on other people's lands."[7]

---

7   Raymond E. Brown, *The Birth of The Messiah: A Commentary on the Infancy Narratives in the Gospels of Matthew and Luke* (New York: Doubleday, 1993), 420.

Shepherds, then, were ruffians who lived on the margins of society. Yet they were among the first to behold God's Son, the Messiah, the Savior of the world. The good news of the gospel was working its grace of transcending margins and creating a new reality. Do not be afraid, shepherds. Do not be afraid, contemporary world. Do not be afraid, Episcopal Church. Behold, I am bringing you good news of great joy for all the people.

Both Luke's gospel and Acts (which scholars say are parts one and two of the same book) emphasize that proclaiming this gospel can produce the spark that transforms individuals and societies. In the fourth chapter of Luke, as Jesus begins his ministry, he identifies his work with Isaiah's prophecy from the days of the exile, a prophecy that envisions the Spirit of God unleashing the good news for all to hear. "The spirit of the Lord God is upon me, because the Lord has anointed me; he has sent me to bring good news to the oppressed, to bind up the brokenhearted, to proclaim liberty to the captives, and release to the prisoners; to proclaim the year of the Lord's favor" (Isaiah 61:1–2). Jesus' declaration of good news starts a chain reaction of personal and social transformation.

In the Acts of the Apostles, the miracle of Pentecost takes place as the Spirit is poured out and then shapes a new community. As people hear the gospel, barriers break down, bridges are built, and the new humanity in Christ begins to emerge.

While I was in seminary, I became friends with a priest from the Church of Uganda. He later served on the staff of Ugandan Archbishop Janani Luwum. This was in the 1970s, when President Idi Amin engaged in wholesale persecution of Christian clergy and leaders. Amin or one of his henchmen killed Archbishop Luwum himself while the archbishop was reciting the Lord's Prayer.

After my friend went back to Uganda, I did not hear from him for years. I often wondered what had happened to him and his family. Eventually a letter came. My friend and his family had managed to escape to Kenya and were safe. After he told his family's story of fleeing in the night and fearing for their very lives, he ended the letter with these words: "Don't ever forget, the gospel can change the world." My friend was right. The gospel can change the world. And spreading the good news of that gospel is the Church's vocation.

Now someone may be thinking, "That is all well and good about spreading the good news of how God reconciles and breaks down the dividing wall—but is it *Episcopalian?*" That question is not necessarily a comment on our supposed "frozen chosenness." That's actually a legitimate issue. I think one way to address that would be to consider our ways of worship. We Episcopalians believe our worship defines us. The principle of *lex orandi, lex credendi*—as we worship, so we believe—lies at the core of Anglican identity.

So what does our worship have to do with spreading the gospel? Think about how our liturgy expresses our attitude toward the gospel. In a service of Holy Eucharist, when we hear the gospel reading, we don't sit down, we stand up. Ideally a deacon—who interprets the gospel to the world and who symbolizes the Church's calling to live the gospel in the world—reads the gospel. Some congregations use elaborately embossed or adorned gospel books. Or they cense the gospel book before the reading. Some train acolytes holding candles and a cross to solemnly process the gospel into the midst of the congregation. The very act of reading the gospel from the center of the church shows just how much the gospel forms our foundation as Episcopalians. We have reverence for the gospel. The good news of God's reconciling love in Jesus lies literally, even geographically, at the center of who we are.

I want to suggest that discipleship, following Jesus Christ as our Lord and Savior, is essentially about a life in community that is centered on and being shaped and inspired by this good news of reconciliation. Consider the voice of the New Testament: "If you continue in my word [the gospel], you are truly my disciples; and you will know the truth, and the truth will make you free" (John 8:31–32). That's the kind of gospel you can preach. And that's the kind of gospel that can change the world. People inspired by that kind of gospel go out and break down the barriers that divide us. They overturn unjust social structures. They make a tangible difference in this conflict-ridden world. I like the saying about Christian discipleship that is often attributed to St. Francis of Assisi: "Preach the gospel at all times, and if necessary, use words."

Of course, to preach Jesus' gospel of reconciliation, to go out and help break down barriers in the world, you need determination and a passionate commitment. One December I presided at a Eucharist celebrating the Feast of Our Lady of Guadalupe. Before we began, a public procession wove its way through the town streets. On a float stood an 11-year-old girl dressed as Mary, the mother of our Lord. The girl stood still and in place on the float for more than an hour during the parade and then continued to stand perfectly still at her post throughout the service. I sat near her in the bishop's chair, and after a while I became concerned she might be tired. When I asked if she needed to rest, she said, "Bishop, I am a bit tired, but I'm doing what I'm supposed to do. So I know I can make it."

That girl taught me something about perseverance and faith, the kind of perseverance and faith that the Church needs. As we focus on the Church's mission of spreading the good news and creating passionate, committed disciples who will make a difference in the world, as we take action to break down the dividing wall and help create peace and reconciliation, we may discover that the difficulties we feared would stifle us have much less power than we thought. We may discover that the ties that bind us together as sisters and brothers in Christ are much stronger than the forces that would rend us asunder.

An old song says it this way:

> If I can help somebody as I pass along.
> If I can cheer somebody with a word or a song.
> If I can show somebody that [they're] traveling wrong,
> then my living shall not be in vain.
>
> If I can do my duty as a [Christian] ought.
> If I can bring back beauty to a world up-wrought.
> If I can spread love's message that the master taught,
> then my living shall not be in vain.
>
> *Refrain:* My living shall not be in vain, then my living shall not be in vain. If I can help somebody as I pass along, then my living shall not be in vain.[8]

We are part of a Church seeking to be a house of prayer for all people. We are part of a Church that is truly one, holy, catholic, and apostolic. We are part of a Church that shares in the mission of God to realize God's dream of

---

8   Lyrics by Alma Bazel Androzzo, http://www.sghistory.com

reconciliation among all people. That is a Church, that is *the* Church I believe we are called to be. So let the walls that divide now crumble. Let the barriers that separate now be cast down. Let God's dream begin to take on form and give us all, all of us, a renewed life!

## CHAPTER SEVEN

# The Savior's
# Not-So-Serene Call to
# Life on a Wild,
# Restless Sea

A great windstorm arose, and the waves beat
into the [disciples'] boat, so that the boat was
already being swamped. But [Jesus] was in
the stern, asleep on the cushion; and they
woke him up and said to him, "Teacher,
do you not care that we are perishing?" He
woke up and rebuked the wind, and said to
the sea, "Peace! Be still!" (Mark 4:37–39)

The Rev. Canon Theodore Wedel, former warden of the
College of Preachers at the Washington Cathedral, tells a

parable that begins with these words: "On a dangerous sea coast where shipwrecks often occur, there was a crude little lifesaving station. The building was just a hut, and there was only one boat, but the few devoted members kept a constant watch over the sea, and with no thought for themselves they went out day and night tirelessly searching for the lost."[1]

As the parable develops, the lifesaving crew members become known for their bravery and commitment. Others join them in the mission. The lifesaving station starts to grow. Then some supporters become concerned about the dilapidated appearance of the station building and the lifesaving boats. They redecorate and spruce things up. They buy modern new boats.

As time goes by, the emphasis of the mission begins to change. They start referring to the lifesaving station as the lifesaving *society*. Instead of going on rescue missions themselves, members of the society hire specialized rescue crews to actually go out to sea. To keep the redecorated station decent and clean, they build another building to house the people who have been rescued. After a while, most have forgotten that lifesaving once was the community's core activity. Those few who do remember—or care—install a symbolic lifeboat in the room where they hold initiation ceremonies for new members.

Other lifesaving stations spring up along the coast, but the same things happen—each one, after a while, becomes a lifesaving society. Canon Wedel ends the parable with these

---

1  The Rev. Canon Theodore Wedel, "A Modern Day Parable." A version of the parable is found at http://www.ecfvp.org/vestrypapers/death-and-resurrection/parable-of-the-lifesaving-station as well as other online sources.

words: "Shipwrecks are still frequent in those waters, but now most of the people drown."

In the biblical imagination the sea is often, as one scholar has written, "a symbol of turbulence and unrest."[2] In Exodus, the Red Sea impedes the way to freedom until God makes a way out of no way (Exodus 14). Jonah prays for deliverance after the sailors cast him into the depths of the sea (Jonah 1 and 2). The poetry of the Old Testament frequently speaks of the Leviathan, the great monster who inhabits the sea, as the source of chaos in God's creation (e.g., Job 41:1; Psalm 74:14; Psalm 104:26; Isaiah 27:1).

The New Testament also features the sea as a place of trial and uncertainty. Paul is shipwrecked at sea (Acts 27:13–44). In Revelation, when John sees a vision of God's new creation, he rejoices that in that new creation, "the sea was no more" (Revelation 21:1). I think especially of the story in the fourth chapter of Mark's gospel that I quote above, in which Jesus orders his disciples to cross the Sea of Galilee at night. Soon the sea, once blue and beautiful, turns troubled, stormy, dangerous, and uncertain. As the disciples battle the waves, Jesus sleeps in the stern. Finally one of the disciples cries out: "Teacher, do you not care that we are perishing?" Jesus wakes up and rebukes the wind and the waves: "Peace! Be still!"— echoing the psalmist's words, "Be still, and know that I am God!" (Psalm 46:10). Then Jesus turns to the disciples and asks, "Why are you afraid? Have you still no faith?" (Mark 4:40).

I love to sing the hymn that says, "Jesus calls us; o'er the tumult of our life's wild, restless sea, day by day his clear

---

2 The New Oxford Annotated Bible (New York: Oxford University Press, 1991), 1,511.

voice soundeth, saying, 'Christian, follow me.'"[3] Maybe you love to sing it, too. But I'd like to change one word in that first line. I'd like it to read, "Jesus calls us; **to** the tumult of our life's wild, restless sea." Because I believe that Jesus calls us not just "o'er" our life's wild, restless sea, but straight into the middle of that restless, terrifying sea. I believe Jesus calls us, if you will, to join the crew of his lifesaving station and get out on the sea, to rescue those who are lost. Jesus does not call us to serve from the safety of the shore; Jesus calls us to serve in the midst of the storm.

Dietrich Bonhoeffer was a Lutheran pastor and theologian who witnessed to the gospel in the midst of the turmoil of Nazi Germany. It was there that he came to view the call of Jesus as a call to a radical discipleship that follows in the way of suffering, the way of the cross. Bonhoeffer believed Jesus genuinely wants us to live the teachings of the Sermon on the Mount, to live the gospel. For his beliefs Bonhoeffer paid the ultimate price; he was executed by the Nazis. Not long before he died he wrote, "The Church is the Church only when it exists for others."[4] Reading Bonhoeffer, I think of Jesus' words: "If any want to become my followers, let them deny themselves and take up their cross and follow me. For those who want to save their life will lose it, and those who lose their life for my sake, and for the sake of the gospel, will save it. For what will it profit them to gain the whole world and forfeit their life?" (Mark 8:34–36).

Jesus calls us to follow him into the midst of the raging sea, to help bring about God's plan and purpose for the world. In the story from Mark, we heard that a "great

---

3   *The Hymnal 1982* (New York: Church Hymnal Corp., 1985), #550.
4   Dietrich Bonhoeffer, *Letters and Papers from Prison* (New York: Macmillan Co., 1971), 203.

windstorm arose, and the waves beat into the boat, so that the boat was already being swamped." Does any of that sound familiar? Could that "wild, restless sea" be a haunting image of our world? I can see it. I can see it in conflicts in places as far away as Iraq, Afghanistan, Israel/Palestine, Sudan. I can see it in the incessant drumbeat of terrorism. I can see it in the plague of HIV/AIDS tearing apart the life of the African continent. I can see it in the dire threat of climate change. I can see it in the divisions that imperil our life as the Anglican Communion, as Christian churches, as a national and a global community. I can see it in the injustices of our immigration policy and practices. I can see it in the reports of so many people living without access to affordable health care, of so many people who lack adequate housing and education, of so many little children still living in poverty. The mission of the Church that would follow in the way of Jesus will always be headquartered at sea.

The Montgomery Bus Boycott in the mid-1950s provided a catalyst for igniting the Civil Rights Movement. Such leaders as Martin Luther King Jr., Edgar Daniel Nixon, Ralph Abernathy, Bayard Rustin, and Glenn Smiley were intent on changing the law and culture of Jim Crow through nonviolent means. But their efforts came with a cost. Nightriders terrorized the streets. Homes of some of the leaders were bombed. Violence and danger were escalating dramatically. The Rev. Robert DuBois, my father's dear friend and roommate in seminary who served at a small African-American Episcopal Church, was nearly beaten to death by opponents of the boycott. The people of Montgomery found themselves in the midst of a raging sea.

In a sermon titled "Our God Is Able," King recalled what happened to him one night several months into the boycott, when the initial energy of the resistance was beginning to wane. He went home after a rally. His wife and baby daughter were already asleep. He went to bed, too, but the telephone awakened him a few hours later. When he answered, a voice on the other end threatened to kill King and his family. Then the caller hung up.

King said by that time he was wide awake. He went downstairs and made a pot of coffee. At the kitchen table, he put his head in his hands. He tried to pray, but all he could do was cry. Tears streamed down his face. He thought, "I'm here taking a stand for what I believe is right. But now I'm afraid. The people are looking to me for leadership, and if I stand before them without strength and courage, they will falter too. I'm at the end of my powers. I have nothing left. I've come to the point where I can't face it alone."

But then something happened. In the midst of the storm that raged around him, King said he started to experience the presence of God as he had never felt it before. He started to hear another voice far more clearly and powerfully than the voice he had heard on the phone or the voice he was hearing in his thoughts. King heard a strong, confident inner voice urging him: "Stand up for righteousness. Stand up for truth. God will be at your side forever." As a result of that experience of the reality and presence of the living God, King did not give up. He pressed on toward the mark of the upward call of God in Jesus Christ (see Philippians 3:14).[5]

Verna J. Dozier wrote in her book *The Dream of God*: "Kingdom of God thinking calls us to risk. We always see through a glass darkly. I will live by the best I can discern today. Tomorrow I may find out I was wrong. Since I do not

---

5    Martin Luther King Jr., *The Strength to Love*, "Our God Is Able" (New York: Pocket Books, 1964), 131–132.

live by being right, I am not destroyed by being wrong. The God revealed in Jesus whom I call the Christ is a God whose forgiveness goes ahead of me, and whose love sustains me and the whole created world."[6]

These are not easy days for our Church or for our world. Sometimes it's hard to know what decision to make, which way to go. But we will not give up. We will not grow weary, even in the midst of the storm. We will not align ourselves with those who shrink and fall back, as the Bible says. We will not be satisfied with being a lifesaving *society*. Jesus calls us to be a lifesaving station, to save those who are lost and drowning, to calm the storm, to follow Jesus' disciples into the midst of places that are disturbing and demanding. God has made us, all the people of the world, into one family. And as sisters and brothers in Christ, we will heed God's summons for us to witness to the gospel of God's compassion, justice, and love, even in the midst of the wild, restless sea.

---

6   Verna J. Dozier, *The Dream of God: A Call to Return* (Cambridge: Cowley Publications, 1991), 141.

## CHAPTER EIGHT

# When Upside Down Is Really Right Side Up

> "These people who have been turning the world upside down . . . are all acting contrary to the decrees of the emperor, saying that there is another king named Jesus." (Acts 17:6–7)

Paul and Silas and their group of Christians are in trouble. Big trouble. They've been riling up the powers that be in the city of Thessalonica by not only witnessing that a man called Jesus rose from the dead, but by also claiming that this Jesus is the longed-for Messiah. One of their listeners has finally had enough already and fumes to the city authorities that these Christians "have been turning the world upside down." He adds, his sarcasm dripping, that "these people" are "saying that there is another king named Jesus" (Acts 17:6–7).

The Thessalonian's words were meant to condemn, but as Jesus' disciples we would do well to take them as the highest compliment. That's because the kind of discipleship to which Jesus calls us is precisely one of "turning the world upside down." In the first century, when the world was right side up, the authorities maintained impermeable walls to institutionalize and legitimize separation. These sociological divisions produced hostility between Jew and Gentile, between slave and free, between male and female, between people of varying tribes. But according to the second chapter of Acts, on the day of Pentecost the Holy Spirit tore down those walls. And people from all countries and tribes together heard the wonderful deeds of God (Acts 2:1–12).

In the tenth chapter of Acts, the Spirit again broke down walls when Peter realized that God does not make distinctions between Jews and non-Jews, but that "anyone who fears God and does what is right is acceptable to him" (Acts 10:35). And in the fifteenth chapter, the first Ecumenical Council opened the doors of the Church to all of God's children who would seek and follow Jesus. The bystander in Thessalonica who was complaining about the Christians was right. These people were turning the world upside down!

In the first century, when the world was right side up, the "haves" had, and the "have-nots" had not. But Acts suggests that those who followed Jesus modeled a new way of being human in community. The second and fourth chapters of Acts say the disciples shared all they had so that "there was not a needy person among them." (See also Acts 2:43–47 and Acts 4:32–37.)

When things were right side up, a man who was born lame and disabled was condemned to live his life begging for alms just to stay alive. But when the apostles Peter and John saw such a man begging for spare change, Peter told him, "I have no silver or gold, but what I have I give you; in the Name of Jesus Christ of Nazareth, stand up and walk" (Acts 3:6). And the crippled beggar did indeed begin to walk. The world was turning upside down!

I keep daily journal notes of things I need to do, along with reflections and quotations. For years I have written in the front of each of my journals the following words sometimes attributed to the late Margaret Mead, the anthropologist and loyal Episcopalian: "Never doubt that a small group of thoughtful, committed citizens can change the world. Indeed, it is the only thing that ever has."

Mead would have recognized those first disciples in Acts as perfect examples of just such "thoughtful, committed citizens" whose witness of faith did indeed change the world. The stories from Acts point us to a deeper dimension of their discipleship. Those first disciples turned the world upside down because Jesus of Nazareth had turned *their* world upside down. They became instruments of God's transformation because they themselves were being formed and transformed as followers of Jesus. Because Jesus had made a difference in their world, they gained the strength and commitment to bring the good news to others.

In 1956 a Quaker named Bayard Rustin and a Methodist minister named Glenn Smiley traveled to Montgomery, Alabama to help organize the city-wide bus boycott that that was helping the emerging Civil Rights Movement gain traction. The Fellowship of Reconciliation, an interfaith peace organization, had sent them to advise the boycott's leaders.

*Rustin and Smiley understood that the philo-
sophical and theological foundations of nonviolence offered a powerful means of social
change. They began to challenge Martin
Luther King Jr. by asking him: Is nonviolence for you just a short-term tactic, or is it
a way of life? They told him that if the movement's leaders employed nonviolence as a
tactic, it might change some laws. But, they
said, if the leaders incorporated the principles of nonviolence into the very fabric of
the way they lived their lives, making nonviolence essentially a rule of life, then the precepts of nonviolence that the Montgomery
Bus Boycott embodied could deeply influence the hearts of Americans and the pat-
terns of American culture. They also warned
King, however, that following the path of
nonviolence could cost him his life.*

*It was out of these conversations, a lot of
reflection, and the soul-stirring experience
of the bus boycott that King made a conscious commitment to embrace Jesus' teachings about nonviolent witness—as found in
the Sermon on the Mount and elsewhere—
and to integrate them with the practice of
Satyagraha, which was Mahatma Gandhi's
specific path of nonviolence. That commitment not only turned King's world upside
down but also up-ended the worlds of many
others whose names are less well-known.
And as we now know, their commitment to
nonviolence did in fact turn America upside*

*down. We have many miles to go as a nation
before we see justice consistently upheld, but
we are a different and better people because
of the nonviolent practices of King and other
leaders.[1]*

I want to suggest that the first disciples of Jesus made a difference because the way of Jesus, the way of the gospel, the way of God became for them not just a tactic, but a path of life that turned their world upside down. And that suggestion leads me to ask: How do we as the Episcopal Church allow the good news of Jesus to turn our own worlds upside down? How do we as the Church universal allow Jesus to up-end us—in order that we in turn might participate in God's mission of turning the world upside down, of transforming this world from the nightmare it often is to the dream we often hope for? How do we help make disciples who follow Jesus, who are passionately committed to turning the world upside down for the cause of the kingdom of God's love?

Of course, our journey is not just an outward one of good works. Our journey must be partly an inward one of a deepened relationship with God and each other in Christ. The nature of the mission to which we are called is echoed in the words of the song, "Let there be peace on earth, and let it begin with me."[2] Spiritual practices such as prayer and

---

1   See Martin Luther King Jr., *Strength to Love* (New York: Harper and Row, 1963), 169: "The experience of Montgomery did more to clarify my thinking on the question of nonviolence than all of the books that I had read. As the days unfolded I became more and more convinced of the power of nonviolence. Living through the actual experience of the protest, nonviolence became more than a method to which I gave intellectual assent; it became a commitment to a way of life."

2   Performed by Vince Gill, lyrics by Sy Miller and Jill Jackson http://www. jan-leemusic.com/Site/History.html

retreat keep us grounded in a continual sense of God's presence and love.

To turn the world upside down, though, we also need compassionate action. But where do we start? It's easy to be so overwhelmed by the enormity of so many needs and problems that we simply give up. Yet Jesus shows us we are not condemned to a purgatory of the way things always are or the way things have always been. We can do it. We can turn the world upside down. Others have done it, and we can do it, too. In the reality of the Spirit of the living God, our discipleship can make a difference.

A few years ago I traveled to Burundi in Eastern Africa, along with several others, to represent the Presiding Bishop at the enthronement of the Most Rev. Bernard Ntahoturi, third Primate of the Anglican Church of Burundi. The country had been mired in a decade of civil war. It was unimaginable to me to learn of the horrendous numbers of people who had been killed in the war. Hundreds of thousands of refugees were still living in nearby countries. Ever since the signing of the United Nations peace accords that ended the fighting, however, Burundi had been working to rebuild from the rubble of war. And the Anglican Church of Burundi had become a leader in that rebuilding.

To me it was clear that Burundians envisioned the new archbishop's enthronement as a potent sign of hope. They received us as Christ's own and invited us to process with bishops from Rwanda, Tanzania, Uganda, Kenya, Congo, and elsewhere. Our procession started from the diocesan office building in the capital city of Bujumbura, which stood as the lone survivor amidst the rubble of buildings and of lives destroyed by so much warfare and bloodshed.

As we crossed the street in procession into the soccer stadium where the enthronement was to take place, we sang "The Church's one foundation is Jesus Christ her Lord" to the tune of "Stand up, stand up for Jesus."[3] At one point I turned around to take a photo of the diocesan office building. It was only a few stories high, but it dawned on me that the building was a striking symbol of this unfamiliar world I had so recently entered. Around the building lay the rubble of war and destruction. Around us stood soldiers of various rebel factions who once had fought each other but now were fellow members of the Burundian army. A sign atop the building proclaimed its name: "Peace House." At that moment, the building appeared to me as the embodiment of hope. I saw clearly that the nightmare of this world can indeed be turned upside down and rebuilt into the dream of God.

Later I asked one of our hosts about the building's history. He said something that made me realize how our actions can transform the world. He said Peace House had been built with funds raised by the United Thank Offering of the Episcopal Church, collected faithfully by many individuals in many different congregations. Margaret Mead said it: "Never doubt that a small group of thoughtful, committed citizens can change the world. Indeed, it is the only thing that ever has."

My friends, our mission as disciples of the Lord Jesus Christ is no less than God's call to change the world. Our mission is not only to change the world, but to share in God's work of turning the world upside down, transforming and transfiguring it from the nightmare it can be into the dream God destines it to be. We've certainly seen challenges

---

3   *The Hymnal 1982* (New York: The Church Hymnal Corp., 1985), #525.

in the past few years. And we'll see challenges in the years ahead. But never forget, *never* forget, that we follow a Lord who carried a blood-stained cross, a Lord who rose from the dead, a Lord who sustains us and who loves us and who will never let us go.

## CHAPTER NINE

# Keep Your Eyes on the Prize, Hold On, Hold On

Peter got out of the boat, started walking on the water, and came toward Jesus. (Matthew 14:29)

A man, walking on the water? That's impossible! That could well be anyone's reaction to this story of Peter walking on the water. But since this is now one of the most familiar stories in the New Testamant, we're almost used to the idea. The story about Peter is actually unique among the gospel accounts of this incident. All four gospels include the story of Jesus walking on the water and calming the raging sea, and all four gospels proclaim the lordship of Jesus Christ in this event (Matthew 14:22–33; Mark 4:35–41 and 6:45–52; Luke 8:22–25; John 6:16–21). But Matthew's gospel is the only one that tells the story of the apostle Peter walking on the water. In this telling, the writer weaves into this miracle of Jesus an essential message about discipleship and the mission of the Church.

Consider what happens. First, in the midst of all that is going on, the wind and the waves and the terror, Peter focuses on Jesus. Let's listen to the story. "Jesus spoke to them and said, 'Take heart, it is I; do not be afraid.' Peter answered him, 'Lord, if it is you, command me to come to you on the water.' He said, 'Come.' So Peter got out of the boat, started walking on the water, and came toward Jesus" (Matthew 14:27–29). That sounds impossible, of course. But as we see, Peter's focus on the master is the key to Peter's mastery of the storm. It was as Peter focused on Jesus, talking to him, interacting with him, relating to him, moving in his direction, that Peter found himself walking on water. Later in the story, when Peter's focus shifted from Jesus to the scary wind and waves, when his focus shifted from trust to fear, Peter stopped moving toward Jesus, and he began to sink, deep down, into the sea.

Bishop Hilary of Poitiers wrote in the fourth century that Peter found himself walking on the water not because he just up and decided he would walk on the water, not because he set out to do something good or miraculous, but because he was "following in the footsteps" of Jesus. Hilary went on to note that, as Peter followed Jesus, he ended up doing what Jesus was doing, walking on the water. Without being aware of it, Peter was beginning to act like Jesus.[1]

---

1  Manlio Simonetti, ed., Thomas C. Oden, gen. ed., *Matthew 14–28* (*Ancient Christian Commentary on Scripture*) (Westmont, IL: InterVarsity Press, 2002), 14.

Richard A. Burridge, dean of King's College, London, in *Imitating Jesus: An Inclusive Approach to New Testament Ethics*, argues that the imitation of Christ, by which he means living out Jesus' teachings and emulating his example, is the essence of what it means to be a disciple, a follower of the Lord Jesus Christ in the community of the baptized. Discipleship is about following Jesus until his footprints and ours become indistinguishable. Burridge adds that when a group of people, baptized and living into the reality of God, truly strives to imitate Jesus by living his teachings and following his example, then an inclusive and diverse missionary community arises and takes form—because people of all kinds will come to follow Jesus.[2]

This is the core, the heart of discipleship. Jesus said: "A disciple is not above the teacher, nor a slave above the master; it is enough for the disciple to be like the teacher, and the slave the master" (Matthew 10:24–25). Peter walking on the water was not a show of magic or razzle-dazzle. Such things, we learn from Jesus' early sojourn in the wilderness, are temptations of the devil (Matthew 4:1–11). Peter walking on the water is about Peter becoming like Jesus, doing what Jesus was doing, participating in God's mission in the world, becoming the hands and feet, the heart and the face, of Jesus. St. Teresa of Avila said it so well:

> Christ has no body but yours,
> No hands, no feet on earth but yours,
> Yours are the eyes with which he looks [with]
> Compassion on this world.

---

2  See Richard A. Burridge, *Imitating Jesus: An Inclusive Approach to New Testament Ethics* (Grand Rapids, MI: William B. Eerdmans, 2007), 182.

> Yours are the feet with which he walks to do
>   good,
> Yours are the hands with which he blesses all
>   the world.[3]

Discipleship is about focusing on Jesus, following in the footsteps of Jesus, becoming his hands and feet in the world. Discipleship is about loving as Jesus loves, giving as Jesus gives, forgiving as Jesus forgives, welcoming and including as Jesus welcomes and includes, doing justice and loving mercy and walking humbly with God, like Jesus. Matthew's gospel concludes with Jesus telling the disciples to "go therefore" and make disciples who make a difference in the world. "Go therefore" and be my hands, be my feet, be my face, be my voice, and change the world! (Matthew 28:19–20).

An old spiritual grasps the importance of this focus, this gaze on Jesus:

> Got my hands on the gospel plow,
> Wouldn't take nothing for my journey now.
> Keep your eyes on the prize, hold on, hold on.
> Keep your eyes on that prize, hold on.[4]

That faith-filled focus on God as revealed in Jesus has implications not only for our individual lives, but also for the life of the Church. Former Archbishop of Canterbury Rowan Williams wrote that the unity of the Church "fundamentally exists in the shared gaze toward Christ, and through Christ to the Father. If we believe that our unity

---

3  http://www.journeywithjesus.net/PoemsAndPrayers/Teresa_Of_Avila_ Christ_Has_No_Body.shtml
4  The authorship of this song appears to be unknown. See http://www. lyrics007.com

comes from that looking together into a mystery and occa-
sionally nudging one another and saying, 'Look at that!' it
can help us feel how the unity we enjoy is not primarily
about institutional uniformity, saying the same words all
the time. The unity is found in the common direction we
are looking."[5]

How do we encourage, energize, and equip ourselves as
the Church to keep our gaze fixed on Jesus, to be the hands
and feet of Jesus in the world, to grow as communities where
we make disciples and send them forth to make a transforming difference in the world? How do we help people
to keep focusing intentionally on Jesus, to keep placing the
gospel of Jesus and his life and teachings at the center of
our lives, to keep following in the footsteps of Jesus? How
do we encourage us all to grow deeper in relationship with
the living God, with the Holy Spirit, through such spiritual
practices as the daily office, centering prayer, retreats, quiet
days, keeping the Sabbath, spiritual direction? This is our
great challenge, our urgent necessity, our high calling.

In Matthew's gospel we see two dimensions to discipleship. We become disciples by following in the footsteps
of Jesus and becoming Jesus' hands and feet in the world.
At the same time, we become increasingly aware of where
Jesus might be calling us to serve him in the world. The
parable of the Last Judgment in the twenty-fifth chapter of
Matthew points to where we can find our Lord's presence in
the world beyond our hands and feet. "Just as you did it to
one of the least of these who are members of my family, you
did it to me" (Matthew 25:40). In the cry of human need, in
the ache of the human heart, in the faces of those downcast,

---

5   Rowan Williams, *Where God Happens: Discovering Christ in One Another*
    (Boston: New Seeds, 2005), 112–113.

and in the lives of those outcast by any human decree or agency—there, in the brother, there, in the sister, we behold the face and hear the voice of Jesus.

To become a disciple of Jesus, therefore, is to follow in his footsteps, to be his hands and feet in the world, and at the same time to search for and respond to his presence in our sisters and brothers. It calls to mind our Baptismal Covenant: "Will you seek and serve Christ in all persons, loving your neighbor as yourself?"[6] Sometimes our response takes the form of what we call outreach and service, sometimes the form of works of justice, sometimes the form of works of compassion, and sometimes it's just a matter of a child of God being a brother or a sister to another child of God. But for us as Christians, it is always a matter of following in the footsteps of Jesus, walking in the way of the gospel, focusing on Jesus, and serving him in others as our witness in the world.

A few years ago when we decided to move our diocesan offices, we wanted to create just such a witness to serving Jesus where we find his presence in the world. The Episcopal Diocese of North Carolina had been headquartered in the suburbs, but we were determined to relocate to the city center of Raleigh. I believe the seat of a diocesan bishop should be in an urban center so the Episcopal Church can make a visible and tangible witness to the gospel. These days, our Diocesan House is just one block from the State Capitol and across the street from an Episcopal parish's soup kitchen. This is not only a strategic investment of our church in the future of the city, although that is part of it. This is also our witness to the gospel. This is one way that we as the Episcopal Church can plant the cross of Christ at

6   *The Book of Common Prayer* (New York: Church Hymnal Corp., 1986), 305.

the crossroads of our state capital, where laws are made and business is transacted. It is part of being the hands, the feet, the presence of Christ in the world.

Jesus said to his first disciples: "You will be my witnesses in Jerusalem, in all Judea and Samaria, and to the ends of the earth" (Acts 1:8). Never underestimate the power of a witness. In the late 1930s a black woman and her little boy were walking down a street in South Africa. A white priest in a long cassock was walking toward them. As he approached the mother and child, he tipped his hat as a gentleman would do in those days when passing a white lady. Years later, the little boy would recall the experience with these words: "You could have knocked me down with a feather. . . . He doffed his hat to my mother. Now that seemed a perfectly normal thing I suppose for him, but for me, it was almost mind-boggling, that a white man could doff his hat to my mother, a black woman, [who was] really a nonentity in South Africa's terms."[7]

The priest was a missionary monk of the Anglican Community of the Resurrection. But that day the hands that tipped the hat were the hands of Jesus. Those hands were responding to the presence of Jesus in this black woman and her black son. That one act of grace and respect had a major impact on the little boy, who would grow up to have a major impact on South Africa. The little boy who was walking with his mother that day would grow up to be the Archbishop of Cape Town, the head of what was known as the Church of the Province of Southern Africa, and a key player in the movement against the injustices of apartheid.

---

7  John Allen, *Rabble-Rouser for Peace: The Authorized Biography of Desmond Tutu* (New York: Free Press, 2006), 26.

The little boy's name was Desmond Tutu. As I said, never underestimate the power of a witness.

I hear in the Letter to the Hebrews our call, our marching orders: "Therefore, since we are surrounded by so great a cloud of witnesses, let us also lay aside every weight and the sin that clings so closely, and let us run with perseverance the race that is set before us, looking to Jesus the pioneer and perfecter of our faith, who for the sake of the joy that was set before him endured the cross, disregarding its shame, and has taken his seat at the right hand of the throne of God" (Hebrews 12:1–2). Let us become re-dedicated, re-consecrated, and re-committed to the work of making disciples of Jesus who will make a difference in the world. Let us become like Peter and fix our gaze on Jesus, so that we may become Jesus' hands and feet in the world.

Then let us go forth as witnesses to the remarkable, reconciling love of God that we know in Christ Jesus. Go therefore, and witness to the justice and the compassion and the forgiveness of God. Go therefore, and help God end the nightmare this world shows us and help realize God's dream. Go therefore, and become the hands and the feet, the face and the embracing arms, of our Lord Jesus Christ in this world.

> Got my hands on the gospel plow,
> Wouldn't take nothing for my journey now.
> Keep your eyes on the prize, hold on, hold on.
> Keep your eyes on that prize, hold on.[8]

---

8 The authorship of this song appears to be unknown. See http://www. lyrics007.com

## CHAPTER TEN

# The Outstretched Arms of Jesus and the Limitless Reach of Love

Now among those who went up to worship at the festival were some Greeks. They came to Philip, who was from Bethsaida in Galilee, and said to him, "Sir, we wish to see Jesus." Philip went and told Andrew; then Andrew and Philip went and told Jesus. Jesus answered them, "The hour has come for the Son of Man to be glorified. . . . Now is the judgment of this world; now the ruler of this world will be driven out. And I, when I am lifted up from the earth, will draw all people to myself." (John 12:20–23, 31–32)

This passage stuns me every time I read it. It offers us as Christians nothing less than the mind of God made plain and the heart of God laid wide open. Let's examine it closely. The events that the writer of John's gospel is relating unfold in the context of Jesus' death on the cross. Only a few days after Jesus said the words, "I, when I am lifted up from the earth, will draw all people to myself," he was arrested, put on trial, and executed.

It is in the shadow of the cross that the author of John includes the detail that the people who came searching for Jesus were "some Greeks." Not only that, but the author takes care to make sure we know that the person to whom these "Greeks" went with their request was Philip, whose name is of Greek origin, and that we further know that Philip was from Bethsaida, a predominately Gentile city on the northeast shore of the Sea of Galilee. To the people in Jerusalem, Bethsaida was far away, way up in northern Palestine.

Could the approach of these "outsiders" have inspired Jesus to interpret the meaning of his death and to claim the purpose for which he came into the world—and for which he was willing to sacrifice his life—with this striking image: "I, when I am lifted up from the earth, will draw all people to myself"?

Who were these "Greeks," and why might they be significant? In his commentary on John's gospel, Raymond E. Brown says the term "Greek" in this and similar passages in John refers to "the pagan Gentiles of the Roman Empire who were influenced by Greek culture."[1] So "Greek" includes those who were Gentiles, not Jews. Greek meant stranger. Greek meant alien. Greek meant uncircumcised,

---

1   Raymond E. Brown, *The Gospel According to John I–XII* (Garden City, NY: Doubleday & Company, 1966), 314.

beyond the covenant, one not chosen. Greek meant heathen, barbarian, and pagan. Greek meant "not one of us," outsider, and sometimes outcast. Some Greeks came searching for Jesus in the context of the shadow of the cross. And Jesus responded, "Now is the judgment of this world; now the ruler of this world will be driven out. And I, when I am lifted up from the earth, will draw all people to myself."

Jesus' words make plain God's deep desire and dream for us, God's plan and mission: to draw all people, to invite, to welcome, to include all within the embrace of those arms that were stretched out "on the hard wood of the cross."[2] As Jesus draws us closer to God, he draws us closer to each other. The Epistle to the Ephesians says that in Jesus Christ, God has now "made known to us the mystery of his will . . . as a plan for the fullness of time, to gather up all things in him" (Ephesians 1:9–10). Or as Jesus said: "I, when I am lifted up from the earth, will draw all people to myself."

You can see this drawing together, this gathering, this inviting, this welcoming mission of God being carried out over time in the grand sweep of the Bible itself. You can see it implied in the second chapter of Isaiah in which the prophet envisions varied peoples and nations flocking to God's holy mountain to hear and learn of God's will, so that God's way leads them to beat their swords into plowshares and their spears into pruning hooks (Isaiah 2:1–4).

You can see God's mission of drawing together, gathering, inviting, and welcoming being carried out in the genealogy of Jesus in Matthew's gospel. The author of Matthew makes a point of noting that the thoroughly Jewish lineage

---

2  *The Book of Common Prayer* (New York: Church Hymnal Corp., 1991), 101.

of Jesus actually included Gentiles such as Rahab of Jericho and Ruth, the great-grandmother of David (Matthew 1:1–17).

You can see this drawing, gathering, inviting, and welcoming work of God in the Epiphany story as the Gentile wise men offer their gifts to the newborn Jewish Messiah. You can hear it in the Gospel of Matthew when Jesus says, "Come to me, all you that are weary and are carrying heavy burdens, and I will give you rest" (Matthew 11:28). You can hear it in the Gospel of John when Jesus says, "I am the good shepherd. I know my own and my own know me. . . . I have other sheep that do not belong to this fold. I must bring them also, and they will listen to my voice. So there will be one flock, one shepherd" (John 10:14, 16).

This impulse fuels the Great Commission in Matthew, "Go therefore and make disciples of all nations" (Matthew 28:19). You can see it on the Day of Pentecost, when people from many nations and tribes all share the same Spirit and hear the same gospel (Acts 2). You can see it in the tenth chapter of Acts where Peter, observant Jew that he is, learns that God's dream is bigger than he ever could imagine and that now Gentiles as well as Jews are included in God's plan of salvation (Acts 10). You can see it when Paul says that among those baptized into Christ, "There is no longer Jew or Greek, there is no longer slave or free, there is no longer male and female; for all of you are one in Christ Jesus. And if you belong to Christ, then you are Abraham's offspring, heirs according to the promise" (Galatians 3:28–29). As Jesus told Andrew and Philip: "I, when I am lifted up from the earth, will draw all people to myself."

The Gospel of John's account of Jesus' crucifixion includes an incredible moment we read about only in John. Jesus is now in the final stages of death. In one last act of consciousness he sees through blood, sweat, and his own tears his mother standing beside him. Near her stands one of the disciples who is sometimes called "the beloved disciple." Summoning the last of his strength, Jesus speaks to his mother. I can see him angling his head in the direction of the beloved disciple as he says to Mary, "Woman, here is your son." And then he turns to the disciple and says, "Here is your mother." The Gospel tells us, "And from that hour the disciple took her into his own home." In that instant a new human family, a new human community, came to be. The writer goes on to say Jesus now knew that all was complete, that the work he came to do was done. He said, "It is finished," and bowed his head and gave up his spirit (John 19:26–30). "I, when I am lifted up from the earth, will draw all people to myself."

When we draw closer to God, we draw closer to each other, for we are all children of the one God who created us all. And when God draws us closer, the Spirit moves, and we experience the power of Pentecost, that day many Christians over the centuries have regarded as the day when the Church was born. Paul said, "If anyone is in Christ, there is a new creation: everything old has passed away; see, everything has become new!" (2 Corinthians 5:17). Let's listen once again to our Lord: "I, when I am lifted up from the earth, will draw all people to myself." Jesus is not talking about a revival. He's talking about a new Church!

I have caught glimpses of what this new Church could look like. In just once such instance, at a service in our diocese at a predominately Latino congregation, I experienced the joy of the shared ministry and support for that congregation that moved across ethnic and racial lines, that included many clergy and congregations and seminaries and dioceses. I saw the outward and visible signs of the deeper and invisible work that God had been doing among us for a while. At services like this, where the broad spectrum of the Episcopal Church is at work, where we share our many gifts and skills and blessings, we join hands and we put our hands in God's unchanging hand, as my grandmother would say. And the result is something beautiful for God—a new Pentecost. A new Church!

What would happen if the Episcopal Church consistently fostered that kind of relationship, support, and shared ministry among clergy, congregations, seminaries, and dioceses? Imagine! The old hymn invites us to "ponder anew what the Almighty can do."[3] What would happen if we worked to foster relationships of mutual support and ministry that connect us to each other in Christ—so that the whole body can grow and develop and witness and serve the world in the name of Jesus?

Something is happening. I'm not talking about a revival, I'm talking about building a new Church. But we have a paradox here. The new Church I'm talking about is not new because it is disconnected from what has gone before. This new Church is not created *ex nihilo*. This new Church is, paradoxically, a reclaiming of the apostolic roots of Pentecost that gave birth to the Church in the first place. This is who and what we say we are when we declare our loyalty to the faith in the words of the Nicene Creed: "We believe in one holy catholic and apostolic Church."[4]

To be a Christian in the catholic tradition of Anglicanism is to be "baptized into one body" (1 Corinthians 12:13). We are incorporated into Christ's body and therefore a part of the whole Body of Christ that is cosmic and universal, that

---

3  *The Hymnal 1982* (New York: The Church Hymnal Corp., 1985), #390.
4  *The Book of Common Prayer* (New York: Church Hymnal Corp., 1991), 359.

spans the globe, that reaches back to the community of saints who are now in the nearer presence of the Lord they served. To be Christian in the catholic tradition of Anglicanism is to be connected, to be in relationship, to be in communion and community in the Body of Christ. We are not independent individuals, neither are we autonomous congregations. We are one Church, the Body of Christ in the Episcopal tradition. "There is one body and one Spirit . . . one Lord, one faith, one baptism, one God and Father of all, who is above all and through all and in all" (Ephesians 4:4–6). That's a complete summation of who we are. And reclaiming that identity is not just a revival. It's a new Church.

Of course, sometimes this kind of drawing together can be uncomfortable for us. Sometimes it is easier when we remain farther apart, when we keep our distances. We tend to seek familiarity by keeping with those who look like us or who act like us or with whom we agree. But those outstretched arms of Jesus on the cross aren't reaching out just to our friends. Not at all. Those outstretched arms of Jesus are reaching out to all, to everyone, to those who "might come within the reach of your saving embrace."[5] They're reaching out to the whole creation.

The Second Vatican Council proposed that part of the vocation of the Church is to be a sign to the world of what God dreams for all creation.[6] I have seen an emerging ecumenical and interfaith consensus on this view of the

---

5  *The Book of Common Prayer* (New York: Church Hymnal Corp., 1991), 101.
6  See *The Dogmatic Constitution of the Church—Lumen Gentium*, chapter 1, "The Mystery of the Church," in *Documents of the Second Vatican Council*, 1964, http://www.vatican.va/archive/hist_councils/ii_vatican_council/documents/vat-ii_const_19641121_lumen-gentium_en.html

Church.[7] We're coming to agree that God's dream does not stop at the door of any one congregation or any one diocese or any one church, or even any one religion. As the Church, part of our calling from our Lord is to join hands with other people of good will and of other faiths to build a social and global order that reflects God's dream and vision for us all.

This vision is a key reason why our Church must commit to the abolition of poverty and the other important work of the Millennium Development Goals. Hunger knows no religion. Suffering knows no color. Injustice and oppression exist everywhere. Poverty submits to no creed. All blood is red. All pain hurts. We all breathe the same oxygen. As the prophet Malachi said, "Have we all not one father? Has not God created us?" (Malachi 2:10). We and all creatures and the environment in which we all live are part of the family of God called creation. Therefore, the work of ending poverty, the work of ending hunger, the work of repairing our environment is the work of God drawing God's creation closer.

During my last sabbatical I rested, spent time with my family, and, despite the fact that I haven't a musical bone in my body, I began taking violin lessons, something I had long wanted to do. The sabbatical created the space and time to step back and reflect. I was ordained a priest in 1978, and I have been truly blessed and profoundly privileged to have

---

7   See Wolfhart Pannenberg, *Systematic Theology, Volume 3* (Grand Rapids, MI: William B. Eerdmans, 2009); John Macquarrie, *Principles of Christian Theology* (Norwich, UK: SCM, 2003); Jaroslav Pelikan, *The Melody of Theology: A Philosophical Dictionary* (Cambridge, MA: Harvard University Press, 1988); Joan Chittister, *In Search of Belief* (Chawton, UK: Redemptorist Publications, 2009); Hans Kung, *The Church* (New York: Continuum, 2001) and *On Being a Christian* (Norwich, UK: SCM Press, 2012).

served the Church. I love our Lord. I love this Church. The sabbatical was an important way station on my journey, because it created some space and time, as that great hymn I mentioned says, to "ponder anew what the Almighty can do."[8] To "have a little talk with Jesus," as my grandmother used to say. This time away created some space to imagine.

I found myself pondering questions that kept coming into my mind. At the end of the day, when all is said and done, "when the roll is called up yonder," I wondered, what really matters? What kind of life am I living? What is the gospel really about? Is Church just a game we play, a show we put on, or is there something really important going on here? I asked myself, what's in my heart? What do I believe, as the song "We Shall Overcome" says, "deep in my heart"?

During that time, what kept coming back to me was that, deep in my heart, I believe that when Jesus said, "My house shall be called a house of prayer for all peoples," he really meant it (Isaiah 56:7, Mark 11:17). When Jesus spoke these words, he was quoting the prophet Isaiah and a portion of Scripture which dreams for the day when those who have long been excluded will be included and when those who have long been cast out will be brought in. When Jesus spoke those words, he had just stunned everyone at the temple by overturning the tables of the money changers. Jesus didn't mince those words. He really meant them. He let them ring out.

From Isaiah, and from Jesus, I experienced in a profound way the truth that God intends for the Church to be a house of prayer for all—fully, truly, equally, completely, all! The theologically conservative and the theologically

---

8   *The Hymnal 1982* (New York: Church Hymnal Corp., 1985), #390.

liberal—all! The politically red and politically blue—all! The Latino, the Native American, the Anglo, the Asian, the African, even the "Greek"—all! The gay person, the lesbian, the bisexual, the transgendered, the straight—all! The poor, the wealthy, and the in-between—all! The Bishop of New Hampshire and the Bishop of Nigeria—all! The insider and the outsider—all! Isaiah said it. Jesus said it. "My house shall be called a house of prayer for *all* people."

I think of my Lord's words just before he was arrested and put on trial and crucified: "I, when I am lifted up from the earth, will draw all people to myself." That to me is God's vision. That to me is God's vision of the Church as the Body of Christ, reaching as far and as wide as those outstretched arms of Jesus. As a child of God, as a baptized disciple of the Lord Jesus Christ, as a human being, as a descendant of slaves in North Carolina and Alabama, as a father and a grandfather, as your bishop and as your brother, this is the vision I believe, God's vision, and I believe it deep in my heart.

"Lord Jesus Christ, you stretched out your arms of love on the hard wood of the cross that everyone might come within the reach of your saving embrace: So clothe us in your Spirit that we, reaching forth our hands in love, may bring those who do not know you to the knowledge and love of you; for the honor of your Name. *Amen.*"[9]

---

9 *The Book of Common Prayer* (New York: Church Hymnal Corp., 1991), 101.

**CHAPTER ELEVEN**

# *E Pluribus Unum:*
# God's Dream, Our Hope

> For in [Jesus] all the fullness of God was
> pleased to dwell, and through him God was
> pleased to reconcile to himself all things,
> whether on earth or in heaven, by making
> peace through the blood of his cross.
> (Colossians 1:19–20)

In August 1587, a man of the Algonquian nation named
Manteo and an infant daughter of English settlers named
Virginia Dare were baptized together at a settlement estab-
lished under the auspices of Sir Walter Raleigh that would
later become known as "the Lost Colony." Theirs were
the first recorded baptisms by the Church of England in
North America. That the first Anglican baptisms in
America, on the shores of North Carolina, should be those

of a Native American adult and the infant child of English settlers is, as they might have said in those days, an intimation of Divine Providence. God's trying to tell us something!

In the seventeenth century John Donne, the dean of St. Paul's Cathedral in London, wrote these words: "The church is catholic, universal, so are all her actions; all that she does belongs to all. When she baptizes a child, that action concerns me; for that child is thereby connected to . . . the body whereof I am a member. And when she buries a man, that action concerns me: all mankind is of one author. . . . No man is an island, entire of itself; every man is a piece of the continent, a part of the main. If a clod be washed away by the sea, Europe is the less. . . . Any man's death diminishes me, because I am involved in mankind; and therefore never send to know for whom the bell tolls; it tolls for thee."[1] The elegant and hopeful vision suggested in Donne's words—the vision of a human family interconnected and interwoven—grew out of Donne's vision of the Church as the Body of Christ, where no one is diminished, all are gathered, and all are cherished.[2]

Donne's idea of the vast interdependence of all beings affirms that we are all needed in this world and all dependent on each other. But the foundation of this idea lies deeper still. This notion of humanity as intrinsically interrelated is deeply rooted in the teachings and the example of our Lord Jesus Christ, and so it is therefore ultimately grounded in the very heart of God. For in Jesus, "all the fullness of God was pleased to dwell, and through him God

---

1 John Donne, *Devotions upon Emergent Occasions and Death's Duel,* "Meditation XVII" (New York: Vintage Books, 1999), 102–103.

2 See John Stubbs, *John Donne: The Reformed Soul: A Biography* (New York: W.W. Norton and Co., 2006), see xix, xxv, and 447.

was pleased to reconcile to himself all things, whether on earth or in heaven" (Colossians 1:19–20). "All the fullness of God was pleased to dwell." The writer of the Letter to the Colossians adds no footnote qualifying this thought, no parentheses circumscribing it, no asterisk mitigating it. In God's world, in God's good creation, 'all' really does mean all!

We see this "fullness of God" exemplified in Jesus's life and ministry; we see that "through him God was pleased to reconcile to himself all things." Jesus' mission throughout his ministry and through his death and resurrection was focused on healing, giving, forgiving, reconciling, and always, always holding up to all he met a vision of the kingdom of God. Of course, Jesus' teachings on forgiveness and reconciliation do not mean that "anything goes," either for the disciples in Jesus' day or for the Church today. On the contrary, the mission community to which God calls us is a community of diverse disciples who have been baptized into the reality of the Triune God and are committed to living their Baptismal Covenant, following the teachings of Jesus, living the way of Jesus, living the gospel, following in Jesus' footsteps as a biblical people, being reconciled to one another as the Body of Christ, and making a difference in the world.

In my travels I often visit just such communities of disciples who are dedicated to following their Lord in whatever way he calls them. One example is an Episcopal congregation I've visited in a small town in the foothills. Some of the people there started sensing that God was leading them to find a way to be faithful to the teachings of Jesus while our nation was at war in Iraq and Afghanistan. They decided to begin where Episcopalians often like to begin, with worship and prayer. When they offered their first "Liturgy for Peace," only twelve people showed up. They had hoped for a larger crowd, but as someone pointed out, "Jesus started with twelve, and he did pretty well." So they kept on meeting. After a while people from other denominations heard about the services and started to join them. The group now meets monthly for prayer, Bible study, and action. They hold a weekly outdoor prayer vigil. They write to state and national leaders and to the media advocating for peace. They have compiled a discussion guide for adult study groups titled "The Prince of Peace: A Christian View of War," which the Baptist Peace Fellowship posted on its website. The group that started off so small now has grown to include Roman Catholics, Baptists, and Presbyterians. It includes veterans from the Second World War, the Korean War, and the Vietnam War. It includes Democrats, Republicans, independents, liberals, moderates, and conservatives. This to me is God's vision of the Church, this is Jesus' vision of discipleship and service.

Honoring the interdependence of which Donne wrote and which Jesus demonstrated in his ministry means creating a Church that is not only hospitable, but a Church in which we show deep concern for everyone. To do that, though, we often have to leave the comfortable places where we are. And that is scary. I, myself, like my comfort zones. But if we leave those comfortable places and dare to reach out beyond ourselves to others, I am convinced that something extraordinary really will take place.

I think of two congregations in a town in the Sandhills region of eastern North Carolina—one Latino, one African-American. These two congregations have reached beyond their known and comfortable worlds and stretched toward each other. With a grant from the United Thank Offering and the backing of friends and volunteers, they have built a new parish house where God is worshipped, children do homework, meals are served, Alcoholics Anonymous groups meet, and people gather to share their lives. And when a fire burned one congregation's main building, both congregations and others came together and helped out. These two congregations have created a community that includes people of many languages, many colors, and many kinds. It's a clear vision of the Body of Christ in all its wondrous humanity and variety, not just on Sundays but on all the days of the week.

Great risks often bring great anxiety, but they also often bring great rewards. I suspect that is why Michelangelo showed the act of creation by depicting the hand of God taking the risk to reach beyond eternity, reaching into time, to touch the outstretched hand of the human being. I am convinced that was what was going on with the birth of a baby 2,000 years ago in Bethlehem. God leaves the celestial home of eternity and takes the risk, the loving risk, to come among us. "In the beginning was the Word, and the Word was with God, and the Word was God. . . . And the Word became flesh and lived among us, and we have seen his glory, the glory as of a father's only son, full of grace and truth" (John 1:1, 14). The eternal Word of God became human flesh and lived among us. When we leave those places of our comfort and dare to reach out to one another, we experience the possibility of something wonderful, something incredible, even something miraculous taking on form and becoming possible.

Several years ago when I was meeting with the Episcopal Church Foundation, someone asked me, "What do you see as the Episcopal Church's greatest challenge?" Without hesitation, I answered: "*E pluribus unum*—out of many, one." John Adams, Thomas Jefferson, and Benjamin Franklin proposed that phrase be included on the Great Seal of the United States in 1776. At the time they were struggling with how to fashion one nation out of thirteen independent and distinct states. Little did they know that *E pluribus unum* would persist over the coming centuries as the great challenge—and the great hope—of the American experiment. Can we, from many, become one?

Is it possible for us to find a deeper unity that can embrace genuine diversity? We can chart the movement of much of American history through the perspective of that challenge. Whether it has been the question of the relationship between the states and the Union; the question of slavery and the Civil War; the question of women and suffrage; the question of civil and human rights regarding race, gender, sexual orientation, and immigration, the ideal of *E pluribus unum* has posed a momentous and often troubling challenge.

We can also survey the history of the world through the perspective of that challenge. Could Israelis and Palestinians, for example, ever someday lay down their swords and shields? Could groups whose enmity goes back for millenniums ever agree to cease their conflict? Could the wolves of the world and the lambs of the world finally, one day, decide to give up their hostilities and just lie down on God's holy mountain together in peace?

*E pluribus unum* poses the same challenge to us as the Anglican Communion and as the Church universal. Is it possible for us as a Church, as communities, as a nation, as a world, to learn to embrace our differences, to learn to respect our diversity, to learn truly to become, out of many, one? The way we approach and begin to meet that challenge ultimately will determine the fate of the Earth.

Dr. Martin Luther King Jr. got it right: "Together we must learn to live together as brothers and sisters, or together we will be forced to perish as fools."[3] To the Church, to the community of Jesus' followers, focusing on this challenge matters absolutely, both to us now and to the generations that follow us.

At the 2008 Lambeth Conference of bishops in the Anglican Communion, we gathered in what we called "indaba" groups. 'Indaba' is the Zulu word for a conference or council of wisdom. Rowan Williams, then Archbishop of Canterbury, described the indaba groups as places where the bishops could "get together to sort out the problems that affect them all, where everyone has a voice and where there is an attempt to find a common mind or a common story that everyone is able to tell when they go away."[4] In our groups we discussed environmental stewardship and the impact in our dioceses of climate change. Those of us from first-world countries had less to say about climate change and its impact than did those from the developing world—who asked us to tell their stories when we went home.

I listened as the Bishop of Kilimanjaro related that the snow-capped peaks of the great Mount Kilimanjaro are melting. The Bishop of Fiji told us his government has been working with Australia and New Zealand to set up contingency plans to help Fiji if the ocean should continue to rise and threaten their homes and businesses. The Bishop of the Solomon Islands made the most eloquent and impassioned

---

3  Martin Luther King Jr., "Christmas Sermon on Peace," preached at Ebenezer Baptist Church, Atlanta, Georgia, and aired on CBC as part of the 7th Annual Massey Lectures, http://www.thekingcenter.org/archive/document/christmas-sermon

4  "Archbishop of Canterbury: Better Bishops for the Sake of a Better Church," *Lambeth Conference 2008 News*, April 23, 2008.

plea. A short, quiet, distinguished man, he stood up in our indaba group and said: "I plead with you who are Americans to help your government to help us reverse the warming of the planet, because our islands are slowly dying. Please help us—if only because we once helped you. My people saved John Kennedy during the Second World War. We have been your friends. These days, we really need you to be ours."

At the opening Eucharist of the conference, we bishops gathered at Canterbury Cathedral, the Mother Church of the Anglican world and the site of the throne of Augustine of Canterbury, the first Archbishop of Canterbury. Canterbury, the holy destination of Chaucer's pilgrims. Canterbury, within whose walls Archbishop Thomas Becket was martyred. As the cathedral choir of men and boys chanted from the psalms of David, 700 bishops in red-and-white rochet and chimere, representing every color and culture and continent on the globe, processed slowly down the center aisle of the nave, up the great steps, through the screen, into the choir. That procession was an intimation of the dream of the Church—catholic, universal, embracing, interconnected.

During communion we sang the words of the hymn, "All are welcome."[5] As I sang, my heart at first was lifted up "to Mount Pisgah's lofty height," as the old hymn says.[6] But as the hope-filled words sank into my soul, my heart started to sink. As we sang "All are welcome," I was struck that, even as we told of God's ideal for us as a Church, the actual reality of our condition as a Church is a long way from that ideal, and far short of God's dream. I thought of some of my brother bishops and friends from churches

---

5   Marty Haugen, http://www.hymn-books.com
6   *Lift Every Voice and Sing II* (New York: Church Publishing, 1993), #178.

in Uganda, Nigeria, and Kenya who were not there, and I thought of my brother bishop and friend Gene Robinson, the Bishop of New Hampshire, who was not there. And my heart sank, even as I sang.

Jesus shows us the importance of our interdependence, no matter how different we are in nationality or race or culture. Jesus inspires us to make disciples who will make a difference in this world. We try to follow his example, to walk in his ways, but we are not yet all the way there. And we're not completely sure how to get there. We often fall short of what God would have us do, both as the Church and as the human family. I think Jesus, though, would tell us that that's all right. The first disciples of Jesus fell short, too. And in spite of their shortcomings, the day of Pentecost happened anyway (Acts 2),

We may not be there yet, but that's all right. Our Lord taught us to pray, "Your kingdom come. Your will be done, on earth as it is in heaven" (Matthew 6:10). We may not be there yet, but that's all right. St. Paul reminds us that "we walk by faith, not by sight" (2 Corinthians 5:7). The writer of Ecclesiastes says that "the race is not to the swift," but to those who persevere (Ecclesiastes 9:11). It's all right. Jesus himself said: "By your endurance you will gain your souls" (Luke 21:19). So we "press on toward the goal for the prize of the heavenly call of God in Christ Jesus" (Philippians 3:14).

This vision of a Church that follows a savior in whom "all the fullness of God was pleased to dwell" and through whom "God was pleased to reconcile to himself all things, whether on earth or in heaven" is always before us. We will not realize such a vision overnight. It will not happen easily. But it will happen; of that I am certain.

Let us build a house where love can dwell
and all can safely live,
a place where saints and children
tell how hearts learn to forgive;
built of hopes and dreams and visions,
rock of faith and vault of grace;
here the love of Christ shall end divisions:
All are welcome, all are welcome, all are
welcome in this place.[7]

---

7  Marty Haugen, http://www.hymn-books.com

## CHAPTER TWELVE

# The Gospel Witness of Welcome Will Rearrange the World

You will receive power when the Holy Spirit has come upon you; and you will be my witnesses in Jerusalem, in all Judea and Samaria, and to the ends of the earth. (Acts 1:8)

The poet Emma Lazarus, a New Yorker whose ancestors had been Jewish immigrants from Portugal, in 1883 wrote the lines that are now displayed at the base of the Statue of Liberty as our nation was still recovering from civil war and immigrants from Europe were pouring in.

> Here at our sea-washed, sunset gates shall
>    stand/A mighty woman with a torch,
>    whose flame
> Is the imprisoned lightning, and her name/
>    Mother of Exiles. From her beacon-hand
> Glows world-wide welcome; her mild eyes
>    command/The air-bridged harbor that twin
>    cities frame.
> "Keep, ancient lands, your storied pomp!" cries
>    she/With silent lips. "Give me your tired,
>    your poor,
> Your huddled masses yearning to breathe free./
>    The wretched refuse of your teeming shore.
> Send these, the homeless, tempest-tossed to
>    me,"/I lift my lamp beside the golden door![1]

Emma Lazarus speaks of what I call the witness of welcome, the power of the act of welcoming to heal, to liberate, to reconcile, to renew, to restore, and to open the door to new futures and new possibilities.

Jesus manifested the act of welcome from the beginning of his ministry. Welcoming and hospitality were so intrinsic to his mission that we can think of the key to Jesus' ministry as the gospel witness of welcome. As Jesus chose his closest disciples, the twelve who would travel and talk and argue and pray with him during his years of ministry, he reached out across ancient walls that people had erected between one another and drew together a diverse circle of followers.

Richard A. Burridge, dean of King's College, London, observes in his book *Imitating Jesus: An Inclusive*

---

1   Emma Lazarus, "The New Colossus."

*Approach to New Testament Ethics* that Jesus' disciples were "a mixed bunch." He adds, "The list of the apostles contains names redolent of the great Jewish leaders from the period of the Maccabees, James and John and Matthew ([Mark] 3:13–19). Yet we also have Greek names like Andrew and Philip. Simon 'the Cananaean' does not mean he came from Canaan, but is a Greek transliteration of the Aramaic *qan'ana,* meaning 'the Zealot' (as translated in Luke 6:15), a freedom fighter or a terrorist depending on one's view-point, who must have sat uneasily alongside tax collectors like Levi, son of Alphaeus ([Mark] 2:14). . . . Add to this Jesus' habit of 'eating and drinking with tax collectors and sinners' [Mark 2:16], it is not surprising that he comes in for criticism about the company he kept."[2]

Biblical scholar Renita J. Weems makes this point even more starkly in a lecture she delivered at Yale Divinity School. Noting, as Burridge does, that Jesus chose disciples from different backgrounds, Weems said, "These two disciples, Matthew the tax collector and Simon the Zealot, represented both ends of the political spectrum of the day. . . . Yes, eleven o'clock [Sunday morning] remains the most segregated hour in America. . . . But how different would the church look today if we realized that Jesus called the modern equivalent of the most right-wing Republican and the most left-wing Democrat to come together and be his disciples?"[3]

Jesus not only called a wide variety of apostles, he healed and spoke and prayed with a wide variety of people. Burridge mentioned Jesus' dinners and companionship with

---

2  Richard A. Burridge, *Imitating Jesus: An Inclusive Approach to New Testament Ethics* (Grand Rapids, MI: William B. Eerdmans Publishing, 2007), 182.

3  Renita J. Weems, *Yale Alumni Magazine,* January/February 2009, 65.

tax collectors and sinners. We also remember Jesus' ministry on behalf of those who hovered on the outside of the culture, those who had been cast out or oppressed or given up for lost, the blind and the lame and the lepers. Think of Jesus drawing close to such outsiders as the Gerasene Demoniac and the Samaritan woman at the well (Mark 5:1–20, John 4:4–26).

Jesus expressed his gospel witness of welcome even after he was crucified and had died and been resurrected and had come back to the disciples one more time, to tell them to go—to *go!*— and make disciples of all nations, baptizing them in the name of the Father and of the Son and of the Holy Spirit (Matthew 28:19). The gospel way of welcome was Jesus' way to bring together all of our incredible diversity and differences into one people, one faith, one Church. And if the gospel way of welcome was Jesus' way, then as followers of Jesus, this way of welcome is our way, our call, our mission.

Now I'm not talking here about building bigger churches. I'm talking about building a better world. The gospel way of welcome is about a gospel witness to everyone, no matter who they are, to envision together and work together to make the world we live in look a little more like the beloved community of Jesus, the dream of God, the in-breaking of God's kingdom.

As I talk about the gospel witness of welcome, I am aware that such language might at first sound rather benign, harmless, like "motherhood and apple pie," something akin to "being nice." But do not be deceived. Welcome is hardly benign. Sometimes the gospel way of welcome can make strenuous demands on those who feel called to follow its precepts.

For example, Egypt's Anwar El Sadat welcomed the efforts of Israel's Prime Minister Menachem Begin to bring peace and justice to the Middle East and in 1979 signed a peace treaty with him. But what happened to Sadat? He was assassinated by those who opposed his gesture. In 1993, Israeli Prime Minister Yitzhak Rabin welcomed the peace initiatives of Palestinian Liberation Organization chairman Yasser Arafat and joined him in witnessing the signing of the Oslo Accords, an agreement to a framework to resolve the conflict between the Israelis and the Palestinians. What happened to Rabin? He, too, was assassinated.

During the Second World War a woman named Miep Gies was working as a secretary. She must have seemed to all observers like a thoroughly ordinary woman. But when the Nazis began to round up Jews to send them to the concentration camps, Gies and her husband Jan hid and sheltered the Jewish family of Otto Frank, who owned the business where she worked. During the time they were in hiding, Otto's daughter Anne wrote the journal entries that would later be published as *Anne Frank: The Diary of a Young Girl*.

We never know what can happen when we feel called to follow Jesus' gospel witness of welcome. Heeding such a call can require incredible courage. Sometimes this gospel way of welcome can lead us to put our very lives on the line. But Jesus' way of welcome can inspire us to keep working to do what is right in a world where too often too much is wrong.

In *Welcoming Justice: God's Movement Toward Beloved Community*, Charles Marsh and John M. Perkins write, "God gathers us into the family of faith not for our own sake, but also that we might welcome justice and build beloved communities for the sake of the world. That is the purpose that drives the followers of the risen Christ. It is the movement of the Spirit that began at Pentecost and has continued in faithful communities of discipleship throughout every generation."[4]

Jesus didn't found an institution, he began a movement, a "movement of the Spirit." He began a missionary movement of people committed to being not members of some social club but baptized disciples in community, following in his footsteps. It was as those first disciples followed in the footsteps of Jesus that the gospel way of welcome opened the doors to a future they could not possibly have imagined.

If you don't believe me, read the Acts of the Apostles. The book begins with the moment just before Jesus ascends into heaven. Jesus tells his disciples: "You will receive power when the Holy Spirit has come upon you; and you will be my witnesses in Jerusalem, in all Judea and Samaria, and to the ends of the earth" (Acts 1:8).

Soon after that, the Holy Spirit comes. Pentecost breaks out. As people hear the gospel, they begin to create a diverse community that embraces profound ethnic diversity. At that point, everyone is either Jewish or a Gentile proselyte who has converted to Judaism. But by the eighth chapter of the book of Acts, the disciples are witnessing in the region of Judea and in Samaria, an area and a people that first-century Palestinian Jews avoided. In that same chapter an Ethiopian diplomat gets on board; Philip notices him, welcomes him, and baptizes him on the spot. In the ninth chapter a Pharisee, Saul of Tarsus, a man who specialized in religious persecution, is on his way to persecute some more Christians but is temporarily struck blind by the Holy Spirit; he joins the group (and later becomes the apostle Paul). In

---

4   Charles Marsh and John M. Perkins, *Welcoming Justice: God's Movement Toward Beloved Community* (Downers Grove, IL: InterVarsity Press, 2009), 17–18.

the tenth chapter a Roman centurion named Cornelius becomes a disciple, too. All of a sudden, full-blown Gentiles, pagans, and other assorted folk start responding to this Jesus. The first Christians definitely hadn't planned for any of this.

Now the disciples found themselves on the verge of doing something for which neither Scripture nor the tradition of their faith had prepared them. Was it possible that God was actually welcoming Gentiles—without making them Jews first? This issue of whether to include Gentiles, or non-Jews, into a movement that had its origins in Judaism threatened to destroy the community. We see the disciples debating this point in the fifteenth chapter of Acts at the Council of Jerusalem. After lengthy conflict and struggle and prayer, after asking what was truly essential to their faith as well as what could still open the way to the future, after listening to all the voices, they came up with not a bland compromise, but a creative possibility. They decided at that council to open the door to the Gentiles. The Acts of the Apostles concludes in the twenty-eighth chapter with Paul arriving in Rome, the epicenter of the Gentile world.

As the first Jewish followers of Christ found a way to welcome the Gentiles, the movement grew and made its witness in Jerusalem, in Judea, in Samaria, and eventually in Rome itself and then in all the world. Realizing the dream of God, the beloved community, the breaking-in of the kingdom became their witness to Jesus in the world. I don't think I am far off historically when I say that if the early disciples had not found a way to welcome the Gentiles, the movement would probably have died within a few generations, crumbling like just another tiny and fleeting Palestinian sect. And had that happened, we Christians would not be disciples of the Lord Jesus today.

The gospel way of welcome opened the way into the future as God dreamed and decreed it. It opened the way in the first century, and it still opens the way into our future in the twenty-first century. Justin Lewis-Anthony wrote in his book titled *If you Meet George Herbert on the Road, Kill Him: Radically Rethinking Priestly Ministry*: "Hospitality is not an optional extra for Christians, an expression among many other possible expressions of the Christian faith. Rather it is at the heart of Christian self-understanding. We are shown how Jesus practiced hospitality to welcome the marginal and the outcast; we are exhorted to be hospitable in turn, for in doing so we show hospitality to Christ."[5]

I can hear people asking, "All right, preacher, that all sounds well and good, but how are we actually going to live out this gospel way of welcome?" To think about that, we might have to look a long way back—back to those early Christians in the Acts of the Apostles. Many theological commentators have suggested that the Church in our day could have more in common with the Church as described in the New Testament than with the Church of the High Middle Ages or even with the Church of the nineteenth and early twentieth centuries.[6]

---

5   Justin Lewis-Anthony, *If you Meet George Herbert on the Road, Kill Him: Radically Rethinking Priestly Ministry* (London: Mowbray, 2009), 103.

6   See Loren B. Mead, *The Once and Future Church: Reinventing the Congregation for a New Mission Frontier* (Washington, DC: Alban Institute, 1991); Brian D. McLaren, *A New Kind of Christian: A Tale of Two Friends on a Spiritual Journey* (New York: Jossey-Bass, 2001) and *Everything Must Change: When the World's Biggest Problems and Jesus' Good News Collide* (Nashville, TN: Thomas Nelson, 2009); Phyllis Tickle (*The Great Emergence: How Christianity Is Changing and Why* (Ada, MI: Baker Books, 2012); Diana Butler Bass (*A People's History of Christianity: The Other Side of the Story* (New York: HarperOne, 2010) and *Christianity After Religion* (New York: HarperOne, 2012); and Harvey Cox, *The Future of Faith* (New York: HarperOne, 2009).

I think these observers are right. The first disciples lived by the teachings of Jesus until his way of welcome became their way. And that welcome opened the door to new possibilities in the future God has in store. I believe this gospel way of welcome is becoming for us as Christians today, and can continue to become, our greatest witness.

So what can the Church in our day learn from the disciples in the Acts of the Apostles? First, we see they ordered their life together around the teachings, life, and ministry of Jesus, until his way of gospel welcome became their way. Acts 2:42, which is part of our Baptismal Covenant, says it this way: "They devoted themselves to the apostles' teaching and fellowship, to the breaking of bread and the prayers." This is the way of Jesus. The Jesus who sat at a table with tax collectors and sinners. The Jesus who said, "I have come to call not the righteous but sinners" (Matthew 9:13). The Jesus who said, "Come to me, all you that are weary and are carrying heavy burdens, and I will give you rest" (Matthew 11:28). The Jesus who said: "My house shall be called a house of prayer for all the nations" (Mark 11:17). The Jesus who said: "The Spirit of the Lord is upon me, because he has anointed me to bring good news to the poor. He has sent me to proclaim release to the captives and recovery of sight to the blind, to let the oppressed go free, to proclaim the year of the Lord's favor" (Luke 4:18–19).

The disciples also followed in Jesus' footsteps as they worked to eradicate poverty in the Christian community. In Acts we learn, "All who believed were together and had all things in common; they would sell their possessions and goods and distribute the proceeds to all, as any had need" (Acts 2:44–45). And as wealthy landowners became disciples, they opened their homes and shared with the poor. Richard A. Burridge writes that the Gospel of Luke "depicts rich property owners joining the believers and using their homes for the church at various points in Acts (see Acts 12:12–18, 16:14–15, 17:12)."[7] Following in the footsteps of Jesus led the disciples to find creative ways to abolish poverty in their midst. It also allowed them to witness to the radical welcome of God, our God who has made this world for all of us to share.

The disciples did something else as a sign of how seriously they took this radical witness. They called and ordained a new order of leadership in the community: deacons. They charged deacons with interpreting Jesus' teachings to the Church, and inspiring and organizing the Church to eradicate poverty and suffering in the world (see Acts 6:1–6). We still need deacons who can help us carry out the mission of Jesus found in Matthew 25 and in the words of Micah: to feed the hungry and to work to end hunger, to clothe the naked, to visit the imprisoned, to welcome the stranger, to do justice and love mercy and walk humbly with our God (Matthew 25:35–36; Micah 6:8). That is one reason I want to see a dramatic expansion of the ministry of deacons in the Episcopal Church. The ministry of a deacon is to help us as the Church move out from beyond our doors, to follow Jesus out into the world. We need deacons as signs of Christ's ministry to the world.

The disciples' ministry was a partnership of the Holy Spirit and human sweat. What did Jesus tell them? "You will receive power when the Holy Spirit has come upon you; and you will be my witnesses" (Acts 1:8). Jesus said this to the disciples just before he departed physically from them, ascending into heaven. It's as though he were saying, "This

---

7   Richard A. Burridge, *Imitating Jesus: An Inclusive Approach to New Testament Ethics* (Grand Rapids, MI: William B. Eerdmans Publishing, 2007), 263.

is what you're going to need in order to follow me into God's future." We have to remember that the disciples didn't have trust funds and endowments. They were not the established Church. They were more sideline than mainline. And yet because of their witness to the radical welcome of the gospel, inspired and propelled by the Holy Spirit, here you are and here I am, two millenniums later. As the old song that my grandmother used to sing goes, "It is no secret what God can do; what he did for them, he'll do for you."

The gospel witness of welcome is alive and well today. I see it at work in such organizations as North Carolina's Episcopal Farmworker Ministry. EFM offers immigration counseling and assistance, emergency food relief, a Head Start program for children of farm workers, classes in English as a Second Language, and a worshiping congregation that during the growing season draws a surprising average Sunday attendance of 600 people. EFM's missionary vision includes worship through word and sacrament and prayer, evangelism, service to others, working for justice, and discipleship that is geared toward making a difference in the world. This ministry is a witness to what the Holy Spirit and human sweat can do. It is a witness to the power of the welcome of God. And in it we can see the very seeds of our future and the gospel's hope for the world. As Jesus said, "You will receive power when the Holy Spirit has come upon you; and you will be my witnesses" (Acts 1:8).

We can also find the gospel witness of welcome—or its opposite—elsewhere, sometimes in more subtle instances. When I first became bishop of the Diocese of North Carolina, our diocesan offices displayed large portraits of those who have served as our bishops. But I noticed that the portraits of the diocesan bishops were hanging in one wing of the building, and the portraits of the bishops suffragan were hanging in another wing. I knew that arrangement was due to the fact that the portraits of the diocesan bishops had been painted and hung first, and the portraits of the bishops suffragan had been painted and hung much later, and that the floor plan of the building made it difficult to rearrange that.

Still, there was an unintended consequence of the arrangement, symbolic but significant. To explain this unintended consequence, I need to discuss a bit of history. The Episcopal Church didn't always include bishops suffragan. The office actually arose out of an attempt after the Civil War to find ways to minister to and provide episcopal oversight for the newly freed slaves. The racially charged social context did not make those efforts easy, especially after the brief period of Reconstruction had ended. With the rise of the Jim Crow era and its new laws that established segregation and two separate cultures, that missionary task became more complex.

A fierce and agonizing debate erupted in General Conventions beginning in 1874 over various proposals about how to minister to the former slaves.[8] The broadly catholic

---

8   Harold T. Lewis, *Yet with a Steady Beat: The African American Struggle for Recognition in the Episcopal Church* (Valley Forge, PA: Trinity Press, 1996), 6. Lewis reviews in detail the debate in General Conventions and throughout the Church. He writes on page 77 that by 1907, with the debate fierce, the Archbishop of Canterbury "confidentially advised the American authorities to withhold a decision until the matter could be considered by the Lambeth Conference of 1908. The General Convention commission studying the proposal, clearly desirous of keeping in line with the imperialistic and racist practices which were gaining sway throughout Anglicanism, corresponded with Anglican dioceses overseas and found that the most satisfactory pattern was supervision by white bishops with natives as assistant bishops." The suffragan bishop plan therefore was implemented with clear concessions to the realities of global colonialism and the American Jim Crow.

character of the Church, which calls for universality and inclusivity in Christ, came into direct conflict with the culture of segregation that was widespread in American society. Eventually the Episcopal Church created the office of bishop suffragan to provide for episcopal assistance in areas of what was said to be church growth. But, as one historian noted: "The office of Suffragan Bishop grew out of the controversy of how to deal with 'colored work.'"[9]

In 1918, two "Bishops Suffragan for Colored Work" were elected and consecrated: Edward Thomas Demby in Arkansas and Henry Beard Delany in North Carolina. Bishop Delany also served in the other two North Carolina dioceses and in the Diocese of South Carolina.[10]

The motive for bishops suffragan was missionary, but the cultural context guaranteed that such mission would be difficult. Church leaders anticipated that at least some of the bishops suffragan would be persons of color, and they placed various limitations on the office. Despite the efforts of some, bishops suffragan were not allowed to exercise canonical jurisdiction and episcopal authority, and they had no vote in the House of Bishops until 1946. When Bishops Demby and Delany died, the office of Bishops Suffragan

---

9   *Ibid.*, 78.

10  The story of Bishop Delany and his family became more well known with the publication of *Having Our Say: The Delany Sisters' First 100 Years*. The book chronicled Bishop Delany's daughters, Bessie and Sadie Delany, an educator and a dentist. The daughters recalled that although their father was a bishop, he had to endure extreme "degradation" as he exercised his ministry. They observed, "He saw the hypocrisy, but he felt that gently, slowly, he was making true progress for himself and for his people, and he was at peace with that." Sarah L. Delany, A. Elizabeth Delany, and Amy Hill Hearth, *Having Our Say: The Delany Sisters' First 100 Years* (New York: Kodansha America, 1993), 116.

for Colored Work ended, although the office of bishop suffragan continues to this day in a restructured form.[11]

Once I became bishop, I wanted to do something about the fact that the portraits of the diocesan bishops and the bishops suffragan hung in different wings, but as I said, the building's floor plan made any changes difficult. When we moved into new diocesan offices downtown, however, I realized we had the opportunity we needed. Now at Diocesan House in Raleigh, we have arranged the portraits of the bishops of North Carolina in the chronological order of their service to Jesus and in their order of succession to the apostles. Now the portraits hang not in any order that recalls Jim Crow, but in the gospel lineage of Simon Peter, Augustine of Canterbury, and Samuel Seabury.

Maybe we can find a parable in this rearrangement of portraits. Maybe our missionary vocation as disciples of the risen Lord, committed to the witness of the welcome of Jesus, is precisely this: to rearrange the picture of the world as it now is into a new configuration of the way God dreams and wills for the world to be. That kind of rearrangement would constitute the ultimate witness of welcome, a witness to the beloved community and the dawning of the kingdom of God.

My prayer is that the words of George Bernard Shaw— words that Robert F. Kennedy liked to quote—will truly become our own: "Some men see things as they are and ask why. Others dream things that never were and ask why not."[12] Why not a world that reflects the welcome of

---

11  James Thayer Addison, *The Episcopal Church in the United States, 1789–1931* (New York: Charles Scribner's Sons, 1951), 297.

12  George Bernard Shaw, *Selected Plays with Prefaces* (Volume 2) (New York: Dodd, Mead & Company, 1949), 7.

the God who created it? Why not a world where people are drawn closer to God and to each other in love? Why not a world where no child goes to bed hungry and where poverty has become not our story but history? Why not a Church that is truly a community of disciples reflecting the welcome of its Lord Jesus who said, "My house shall be called a house of prayer for all people" and who said, "You will receive power when the Holy Spirit has come upon you; and you will be my witnesses" (Matthew 21:13; Acts 1:8)? Why not a Church dedicated to the witness to which Jesus calls us? The gospel witness of welcome can rearrange the world from the nightmare it often is into the dream God intends for it to be.

## CHAPTER THIRTEEN

# Come, Let Us Go to Galilee—Probably the Last Place We Want to Be

The angel said to the women, "Do not be afraid; I know that you are looking for Jesus who was crucified. He is not here; for he has been raised, as he said. Come, see the place where he lay. Then go quickly and tell his disciples, 'He has been raised from the dead, and indeed he is going ahead of you to Galilee; there you will see him.'" (Matthew 28:5–7)

Jesus is not here; he has risen from the dead! The power of God has conquered the forces of death! The love of God has defeated the hatreds of humanity! "The powers of death have done their worst, but Christ their legions hath dispersed."[1] Jesus lives!

We know that first part of the angel's message so well. What we often miss, though, is the second part of the message, that Jesus "is going ahead of you to Galilee; there you will see him." As important as the first part is, I believe it's time for us to consider more deeply the second part of the angel's message. I believe the angel is saying something about this place called Galilee that is more than mere geography, something for you and me to learn, something for us as a Church to discover.

What do we know about the place called Galilee? I have to admit I've always treasured John Greenleaf Whittier's hymn, "Dear Lord and Father of mankind, forgive our foolish ways!" The third verse says: "O Sabbath rest by Galilee!/O calm of hills above,/where Jesus knelt to share with thee/the silence of eternity interpreted by love!"[2]

I love the hymn, but I'm not sure how accurate it was about Galilee. I'm not sure peaceful hills really describe first-century Palestinian Galilee any more than they describe twenty-first-century Galilee. A Public Broadcasting System documentary titled "From Jesus to Christ: The First Christians" included this information: "While often portrayed as a bucolic backwater, Galilee

---

1   *The Hymnal 1982* (New York: The Church Hymnal Corp., 1985), #208.
2   *The Hymnal 1982* (New York: The Church Hymnal Corp., 1985), #652.

was known for political unrest, banditry, and tax revolts."[3]
It turns out that first-century Galilee was a hotbed of
economic uncertainty, political instability, and cultural
confusion. Scholars and archeologists also tell us that
Galilee in biblical times included a diverse mix of people,
ethnically and economically and religiously—Palestinian
and Hellenistic Jews; Gentiles of Roman, Greek, and
Palestinian origin; wealthy landowners; and the first-
century equivalent of sharecroppers.[4] Galilee was a place
of social and political unrest, often the breeding ground
for rebellions against Rome. It was a volatile environment,
a place of anxiety and fear.

It's to such a volatile and diverse region that Jesus goes
to begin his ministry. It's not an accident that he headed
straight to his home synagogue in Nazareth of Galilee to
preach his first sermon and quote the words of Isaiah: "The
Spirit of the Lord is upon me, because he has anointed me
to bring good news to the poor" (Luke 4:18). It's not an accident that he preached the Sermon on the Mount in Galilee
(Matthew 5–7). It's not an accident that he spent most of his
time in the rural villages of lower Galilee with those who
were "the other," with those on the margins of society and
sometimes on the margins of hope.

---

3   Frontline: "From Jesus to Christ: The First Christians," http://www.pbs.org/
    wgbh/pages/frontline/shows/religion
4   The prophet Isaiah referred to the Galilee of his time as the "Galilee of the
    Gentiles" (Matthew 4:15; Isaiah 9:1). One biblical scholar says, "The name
    [Galilee of the Gentiles] reflects the popular reputation for racial variety
    and mixture in and around these northern frontier districts" of Palestine"
    (*The Interpreter's Dictionary of the Bible, Volume 1, E–J* [Nashville: Abingdon
    Press, 1962], 345). Another scholar describes Galilee in the time of the
    New Testament as an area inhabited by a "multiethnic populace" (*The
    Interpreter's Dictionary of the Bible, Volume 2, D–H* [Nashville: Abingdon
    Press, 2007], 515).

It's not an accident that the angel tells the disciples to go to Galilee to see Jesus again (Matthew 28:5–7). And it's not an accident that Jesus sends his disciples out on their apostolic mission from Galilee with these words ringing in their ears: "Go therefore and make disciples of all nations" (Matthew 28:19). After the resurrection Jesus doesn't stay with Mary Magdalene, to quote the old hymn, in the "garden alone, while the dew is still on the roses."[5] Instead, Jesus leaves the garden and returns to Galilee, to all of its ambiguity, instability, and volatility. And to those who would be his disciples, Jesus says, "Let us go to Galilee."

I want to suggest that the uncertainty, the unpredictability, the anxiety of first-century Galilee make it an appropriate metaphor for the missionary moment that is emerging all around us today. That's because, whether we're talking about global economic and political instability or our own personal uncertainty, we are in Galilee. Whether we're talking about the threat of terrorism or the nightmare of natural disasters, we are in Galilee. Instability, uncertainty, increasing polarity among people because of their ideology or their culture, all these conditions describe our time. We are, all of us, in Galilee.

Social commentators such as Thomas L. Friedman confirm we are in the midst of a massive global cultural transition in everything from our economics to our politics to our faith.[6] Just one example of today's volatility is the rapid technological change we're experiencing. In the fifteenth century, Johannes Gutenberg's printing press provided

---

5   *Lift Every Voice and Sing II* (New York: Church Publishing, 1993), #69.
6   See Thomas L. Friedman, The Lexus and the Olive Tree (New York: Picador, 2012) and *The World Is Flat: A Brief History of the Twenty-First Century* (New York: Farrar, Straus & Giroux, 2005).

the catalyst that spurred the Protestant Reformation, the rise of European nation-states outside of papal control, the Enlightenment, and the Industrial Revolution. These days we have such latter-day Gutenbergs as Steve Jobs, Bill Gates, and Facebook's Mark Zuckerberg. If you're like me, you thought you were up to date when you learned to use email. Then you had to learn to text. Then texting wasn't enough; you had to learn to tweet. A few years ago I was telling churches they had to get a good webpage. Now you've also got to get your congregation on Facebook and make sure people "Like" it. I don't know what will come next, but I'm sure we'll be running to catch up with it soon.

A professor of management studies recently told me that the pace of technological, global, and societal change is so fast that most things that are new in our culture become obsolete in three years or less. We are living through a major time of human transition and transformation, of instability and uncertainty that is no less earth-shaking than that of Gutenberg's fifteenth century. In a phrase, we are in Galilee.

The Pew Forum on Religion & Public Life in 2010 published a report titled "Religion Among the Millennials." They discovered a sharp and dramatic decline in religious affiliation among the Millennial Generation, those born after 1981.[7] Worldwide Christendom is no more.

When Americans are surveyed, do you know what is the single fastest growing religious designation? It's not Islam. It's not Buddhism. It's not Hinduism, Judaism, or any Christian denomination. In fact, since 1990 the percent of people who identify themselves as Christian has decreased

---

7 "Religion Among the Millennials," http://www.pewforum.org/Age/Religion-Among-the-Millennials.aspx

from 86 percent to 76 percent in 2009. The fastest growing religious designation by which people identify themselves is "unaffiliated" or "none," depending on how the question is asked. The percentage of people identifying themselves as "unaffiliated" has doubled since 1990 to more than 15 percent of the U.S. population.[8]

If you don't believe the statistics, go to Starbucks at 10:30 on a Sunday morning, even in the Bible-belt South. Chances are, you won't be able to find a table. A while back I was driving with a priest to church on a Sunday morning. As we passed a mega-church, we started talking about church growth. She said, "Do you want to know what the real competition to our churches is? Just look out the window." I looked out, and at 9:00 on Sunday morning we saw a large field dotted with hundreds of children not headed for Sunday School, but playing soccer.

Once when I was attending a bishops' meeting, a few of us decided to grab a cup of coffee. We walked out of the cathedral complex and only then realized we didn't know where to go. This was in the college area of town, so there had to be a coffee shop somewhere, with maybe some scones and Wi-Fi. But where?

A young man was walking toward us, so we asked him. He thought for a moment, then said he'd show us the way. One of the bishops joked to the young man, "You see, we're a bunch of bishops on an evangelism mission." As we bishops laughed, the young man's faced stayed blank. He didn't get the joke. He had no idea that four guys in clerical collars and purple shirts, with crosses dangling on gold chains, were bishops. Maybe he didn't even know the word 'evangelism.' The young man who didn't recognize a bishop when

---

8   Jon Meacham, "The End of Christian America," *Newsweek*, April 3, 2009.

he saw one may well represent the wave of the American future. He's not an aberration. More and more, he is the norm. At that moment, I realized I was in Galilee.

This trend I'm talking about has nothing to do with liberal church or conservative church. It's affecting mainline churches, mega-churches, all religious institutions. The cultural landscape of America is changing. Ethnic diversity and religious pluralism were characteristics of first-century Galilee, just as they are characteristics of our twenty-first-century Galilee. My grandparents from Hertford County, North Carolina, wouldn't recognize today's landscape either ethnically or religiously. But diversity and pluralism are what we know.

This is not a passing season, but a widespread shift. And the question we face is: What can we as the Church do—for the sake of the gospel of Jesus—to engage this moment? I found a fascinating note in the Pew Forum report. The researchers said that, even though the Millennial Generation has the lowest level of religious affiliation of any generation in history, their interest in spiritual practice and their curiosity about the spiritual journey is much higher than that of their elders. In fact, the level of spirituality among the young adults in this most technologically and scientifically sophisticated generation almost equals the level of spirituality of "the Greatest Generation," those who endured the Great Depression and World War Two.[9]

But how do we engage this complex new mission field, where we find such instability and uncertainty and increasing polarity and declining religious affiliation,

---

9 "Religion Among the Millennials," http://www.pewforum.org/Age/Religion-Among-the-Millennials.aspx

mixed in with some evidence of an increased interest in the spiritual journey?

Now I'm not suggesting everyone has to become Episcopalian, or that we need to ramp up recruitment efforts to fill the pews. That's not where I'm going with this. But I don't for one moment believe that the Lord God put us on this earth just to eat, drink, and be merry. We are here to do more than just consume the oxygen. We are here, as the Jewish tradition of *tikkun olam* teaches, to heal and repair the creation. We are here to love the God who created us and to love and care for each other as children of the one God, as the human family of God. We are here to transform what often is a nightmare of sin and death, hatred and violence, animosity and bigotry into something more closely resembling God's dream of a renewed and transformed human family and creation. I believe that our hope as the human family depends on our getting that right.

I didn't figure that out on my own, though. That's the message of Jesus. That's the gospel. And I believe the world—in the first century and in the twenty-first century—needs that wisdom. But I also believe it's going to be more and more difficult to help that message be heard. And that's why Jesus the Galilean matters.

I would like to suggest a way for us to follow Jesus into the very heart of our contemporary mission field—with all of its anxiety and uncertainty, but also with its incredible potential. The twenty-sixth chapter of Matthew includes a text for our time, a text that can help us help people hear the gospel message. In that story, the Last Supper has ended. The final hymn has been sung. The die has been cast. The betrayer has done his diabolical work. Temple police and Roman soldiers have done their job. Jesus the Galilean, as he was often called at the time, is under arrest, soon to be tried for blasphemy against religion and sedition against the Roman Empire. And his closest followers have fled for their lives.

Simon Peter, now on the run, is trying to hide out. Let's pick up the text from there.

> Now Peter was sitting outside in the courtyard. A servant-girl came to him and said, "You also were with Jesus the Galilean." But he denied it before all of them, saying, "I do not know what you are talking about." When he went out to the porch, another servant-girl saw him, and she said to the bystanders, "This man was with Jesus of Nazareth." Again he denied it with an oath, "I do not know the man." After a little while the bystanders came up and said to Peter, 'Certainly you are also one of them, for your accent betrays you." (Matthew 26:69–73)

"For your accent betrays you." They didn't have photo IDs back then. No Facebook. No LinkedIn. You couldn't even do a Google Image search. But they had ways of finding out who somebody was. Remember, they were in Jerusalem, in southern Palestine. Galilee was up north. A Galilean accent would stand out in Jerusalem like a Brooklyn accent would attract notice in Tuscaloosa. Peter's Galilean accent betrayed him—and exposed him as a follower of Jesus. I wonder if Matthew tells this story to get us to see precisely that—that when people spend time with Jesus the Galilean, their very speech, their very lives will reveal they are his disciples.

Years ago I heard Dr. David H.C. Read, who was then senior pastor of the Madison Avenue Presbyterian Church in New York and one of the great preachers of the twentieth century, preach on this text. I remember how he ended the sermon. Recalling his days as a child in the Church of Scotland, he recited a poem he learned in church school:

> O that it might be said of me,
> Surely thy speech betrayeth thee,
> Thou wast with Jesus of Galilee.[10]

It is that voice, that Spirit, that presence, that life-giving reality of Jesus that can speak anew to our hearts and then through us, if we use its accent, through us straight into the heart of Galilee. Remember, the servant girl said accusingly to Peter, "You also were with Jesus the Galilean." When we spend time with Jesus, our accent is going to betray us. The voice of Jesus of Galilee that spoke and resonated in the first century will speak through us, in the same Galilean accent, in the twenty-first century.

As a Church we can explore ways to take on the accent of Jesus and allow it to form within us. As a Church we can draw nearer and go deeper with Jesus, in prayer and reading and wrestling with the Holy Scriptures, both in the sacred solitude of our spirits and also together, as the community of Jesus, the Body of Christ. I want to encourage us to take our prayer and our reading and our wrestling out beyond the church doors and out into the mission field that God has given us, out into our twenty-first-century Galilee.

Now taking our Jesus-accented selves out to the world

---

10  As I mentioned, I first heard this poem in a sermon preached by the Rev. David H.C. Read and broadcast on "The Protestant Hour" in the late 1970s. I have been unable to find the manuscript of the sermon, and I share these lines from memory.

might sound a little scary to some of us. But for inspiration, I'm reminded of the words of Dietrich Bonhoeffer, the theologian and pastor whom the Nazis imprisoned and executed for opposing the Third Reich. Writing from his prison cell, Bonhoeffer called Jesus quintessentially the one "for others."[11] Jesus calls and challenges those of us who would follow in his footsteps to be a people and a community reaching out above and beyond our own self-interest. Jesus said, "The Son of Man came not to be served but to serve, and to give his life a ransom for many" (Matthew 20:28). Jesus is calling us to follow in his footsteps by being a Church for others.

I found an interesting fact about the word 'galilee' itself (when the letter 'g' is lower case). Here's the dictionary definition of 'galilee': "a porch or vestibule, often on the ground floor of a tower, at the entrance of some English churches."[12] So the word 'galilee' can refer to a threshold between the church building and the world, a place of stepping out into the world. The Church in and for Galilee is a missionary Church focused outward, stepping outward.

As we follow Jesus to Galilee, let's think more broadly about being the Church that doesn't wait for the world to come to it but instead follows Jesus out into the world. How might this perspective change the shape of the Church as we seek to witness in the world? In years to come, will the Episcopal Church include only the parishes, missions, campus ministries, and institutions that we have now? Or will we encompass many varied forms of expression in

---

11   Dietrich Bonhoeffer, *Letters and Papers from Prison* (New York: Macmillan Publishing Co., 1972), 381.

12   *The Random House College Dictionary* (New York: Random House, 1984), 540.

our Episcopal tradition, including house churches or even churches out on the streets? What would happen if we encouraged new possibilities for being worshipping and serving communities? What would an Episcopal Church presence on the street and in public spaces and in non-traditional contexts look like? How could we as the Church foster those kinds of experiments?

A Boston congregation called The Crossing might provide one answer. Housed at the Cathedral Church of St. Paul, the congregation reaches out to young adults in significant—and unusual—ways. They aren't buying land or building more buildings. They're using the resources they already have to proclaim and share the gospel. Instead of waiting for young adults to come to them, The Crossing is going where the young adults are. They're leading people back to the deep Christian roots of prayer, meditation, sacrificial service, and witness to the gospel in the world. They're recovering the spiritual disciplines of the ancient Church, of the gospel, of the risen Christ in Galilee.

I hear of congregations in the Church of England that also are no longer waiting for young people to return to church after they get married and have children. The Church is going to them where they are, spurred on by the "Fresh Expressions" movement which encourages congregations to reach out to new generations in innovative ways.

But we're not just talking about ministry to young adults. We're talking about ministry to every kind of person in our modern-day Galilee. Let me tell you about a parish in a small North Carolina town that embodies this mission. Every Thursday at noon you'll see what you might at first think is a soup kitchen to feed the poor. But this soup kitchen has a remarkable twist. It's for everybody, and I mean everybody: homeless, homebound, business folk, farmers, artists, Republicans, Democrats, rich, and poor. When I visited there I was reminded of that old spiritual: "I'm gonna come to the welcoming table one of these days." That's the radical welcome of Jesus. That's a Church for others.

I'm convinced our missionary goal at this time is not to build bigger churches or start a lot of new churches or fill up the pews. I'm not convinced those in themselves are goals born of the gospel. They might have more to do with institutional survival, with the idea that bigger is better. I am convinced, however, that our missionary goal as a Church is to live, witness to, and share the gospel of Jesus Christ in order to make disciples—disciples who will join us in making a real difference in the world for the cause of God's kingdom and the realization of God's dream. That is a missionary goal born of the gospel, suited for our time, and worthy of our effort. We are living in a new mission context. For an emerging population, the gospel of Jesus will not be just the good news. It will be the *new* news.

We now have an opportunity to look deeply and seriously into what it means to be the Episcopal Church, what it means to be faithful and effective in this twenty-first-century context. Yet many, perhaps most, congregations in the Episcopal Church are feeling the strain of this present moment. The missionary challenge before us is bigger than any one of us, or any one congregation. It can seem daunting. We might well feel overwhelmed before we even begin.

A while back my wife and I went to see the film "The King's Speech." It tells the story of how George, the Duke of York, who was second in line to the throne of England, suddenly was called to become King of England after his older brother, Edward, abdicated his right to the throne.

I knew the story. But I had forgotten about the dark clouds that hung over Europe and much of the world at that time as armies of the Third Reich slowly, steadily, and then swiftly and decisively conquered nation after nation, until Europe was covered in darkness and the very survival of civilization was at stake. Sudetenland, Austria, Czechoslovakia, Poland, the European Lowlands, Dunkirk, and France all fell to Nazi occupation. Finally, nothing but England stood between Nazism and the world. It was in that hour that a man who never expected to become King of England was called by historical circumstance to the throne. But he was not prepared. And he stuttered. Like Moses in the Bible, he stuttered.

At one point in the film, when the soon-to-be-king is beginning his speech therapy sessions, he takes out a cigarette. The Australian speech therapist, breaching all rules of etiquette, tells him, "No smoking here. Put that thing out." To which George replies, "My doctors tell me that smoking is good for my lungs." The therapist replies, "Your doctors are idiots." George harps, "They have all been made knights." The therapist retorts, "Well then, that makes it official."

Their relationship is the film's story. I watched, fascinated, as these two fallible human beings worked together, one with the skill of a therapist of speech and a therapist of the soul, and the other with the urgent need to summon incredible courage to find his voice as the voice of a king.

Before I went to the movie I had known the broad strokes of the historical story, and I love history. But I hadn't expected to be so moved. I was moved because King George was a man who didn't think he had what it took to lead his nation through its most difficult hour. Still, through his work and through his relationship with the speech therapist, a miracle happened. It wasn't that George suddenly turned into his brother Edward, the one who had been groomed to be king. The miracle was that the real George, deep inside, was allowed to emerge. And when the authentic George did emerge, it became clear that his was exactly the voice that was needed. England hadn't known it at the time, George hadn't known it at the time, but the king already had within himself the voice he needed, and the voice his country and the world needed, for that hour. His was the voice that became a sign of hope for the British when they stood alone, the voice that became a sign of hope for civilization and for human decency when few other voices were willing or able to be raised.

I wonder if we in the Episcopal Church today aren't more or less in the same shoes as King George. Our mission field is becoming increasingly complex and uncertain. The economics of being a sustainable congregation can be discouraging. We don't have mega-churches, and in fact most of our churches are small. Our funds and resources are limited. On top of all that, we Episcopalians are not generally inclined to give voice to the faith that is in us. We might not feel quite equal to the challenge of our twenty-first-century Galilee. On some level we would like to go back to the "good old days," whenever they were, when things weren't as complex, ambiguous, and uncertain.

And yet, and yet—there is something rich and strong and good and holy within this church. It may be that deep within us and among us we know we already have exactly what we need for this hour. Maybe we just need the Spirit to help us to name it, claim it, and proclaim it with our lips and in our lives.

I remember people in my grandmother's church used to say, "I may not know what the future will hold, but I know who holds the future." Our task now is to follow in the footsteps of Jesus, who on the cross gave himself totally over to God when he declared, "Father, into your hands I commend my spirit" (Luke 23:46). And now, into Jesus' own hand, we commend the Church.

There's an old song that many different people have sung, people like Joan Baez, Shirley Caesar, Ray Conniff, the Five Blind Boys of Alabama, Tennessee Ernie Ford, Ramsey Lewis, the Platters, Loretta Lynn. You probably know it. The words go like this:

> Put your hands in the hand of the man who
>    stilled the water
> Put your hands in the hand of the man who
>    calmed the sea
> Take a look at yourself and you can look at
>    others differently
> Put your hands in the hand of the man from
>    Galilee.[13]

Maybe we already have what we need. A God to worship. A loving and liberating Lord to follow. A gospel that is good news to proclaim. A way of being Christian that is faithful and orthodox, loving and compassionate, open and generous, alive to the mystery of God. A way of following Jesus that is radically welcoming toward all, radically committed to serving the downtrodden and the oppressed, and

---

13  Lyrics by country singer and songwriter Gene MacLellan, http://www. allmusic.com

radically unafraid to proclaim, as the saying goes, that "God loves you, no exceptions!"

A Church witnessing to these extraordinary truths has a message for this moment. This is the truth for the twenty-first century. This is a voice for these times. This is, in fact, the accent of Galilee.

At stake for us is nothing less than the future witness of the Episcopal way of being Christian. It's a way that dares to be the Body of Christ in the world, that dares to place its future in the hand of the man from Galilee. Come with me, come put your hand in our Lord's hand, and let us go with Jesus to Galilee!

# Appendix
# of Addresses

Chapter 1—Delivered July 7, 2012 at the 77th General Convention of the Episcopal Church

Chapters 2 and 3—Delivered February 2, 2001 to the 185th Annual Convention of the Episcopal Diocese of North Carolina

Chapter 4—Delivered January 31, 2002 to the 186th Annual Convention of the Episcopal Diocese of North Carolina

Chapter 5—Delivered January 25, 2003 to the 187th Annual Convention of the Episcopal Diocese of North Carolina

Chapter 6—Delivered January 30, 2004 to the 188th Annual Convention of the Episcopal Diocese of North Carolina

Chapter 7—Delivered January 21, 2005 to the 189th Annual Convention of the Episcopal Diocese of North Carolina

Chapter 8—Delivered January 26, 2006 to the 190th Annual Convention of the Episcopal Diocese of North Carolina

Chapter 9—Delivered January 26, 2007 to the 191st Annual Convention of the Episcopal Diocese of North Carolina

Chapter 10—Delivered January 18, 2008 to the 192nd Annual Convention of the Episcopal Diocese of North Carolina

Chapter 11—Delivered January 23, 2009 to the 193rd Annual Convention of the Episcopal Diocese of North Carolina

Chapter 12—Delivered January 22, 2010 to the 194th Annual Convention of the Episcopal Diocese of North Carolina

Chapter 13—Delivered January 21, 2011 to the 195th Annual Convention of the Episcopal Diocese of North Carolina and January 20, 2012 to the 196th Annual Convention of the Episcopal Diocese of North Carolina